Getting Things Done in Today's Organizations

The Influencing Executive

Marvin R. Gottlieb

QUORUM BOOKS
Westport, Connecticut • London

Library of Congress Cataloging-in-Publication Data

Gottlieb, Marvin R.
    Getting things done in today's organizations : the influencing
executive / Marvin R. Gottlieb.
        p.   cm.
    Includes bibliographical references and index.
    ISBN 1–56720–214–4 (alk. paper)
    1. Executive ability.   2. Industrial efficiency.
3. Organizational effectiveness.   I. Title.
    HD38.2.G68   1999
    658.4'092—dc21   98–51674

British Library Cataloguing in Publication Data is available.

Library of Congress Catalog Card Number: 98–51674
ISBN: 1–56720–214–4

First published in 1999

Quorum Books, 88 Post Road West, Westport, CT 06881
An imprint of Greenwood Publishing Group, Inc.
www.quorumbooks.com

Printed in the United States of America

The paper used in this book complies with the
Permanent Paper Standard issued by the National
Information Standards Organization (Z39.48–1984).

10 9 8 7 6 5 4 3 2 1

Copyright Acknowledgments

The author and publisher gratefully acknowledge permission for use of the following material:

Tables 3.1 and 3.2 originally appeared as Tables 1 and 2 in David Kipnis, Stuart M. Schmidt, and Ian Wilkinson, "Intraorganizational Influence Tactics: Explorations in Getting One's Way," *Journal of Applied Psychology* 65, no. 4 (1980): 440–452. Copyright © 1980 by the American Psychological Association. Reprinted with permission.

Contents

Illustrations

Preface

THE CHICKEN PRINCE—A FABLE FOR THOSE WHO WOULD INFLUENCE

Once upon a time in a far-off land there was a peaceful kingdom. The King was kind and just, the Queen was loving and charitable, and the Prince—who would be King someday—was growing strong and wise. He was considered the jewel of the kingdom, the most valuable treasure. To ensure his development, the Prince had the finest teachers and the wisest soothsayers to instruct him in all that he would need to know to be a great King.

One day, for seemingly no reason, the Prince began acting strangely. He thought he was a chicken. He took off all his clothes and roamed around the palace flapping his arms and making clucking noises. He stopped speaking in normal language altogether, and would not eat with others. He would get down on the floor under the great table to peck corn from the floor.

Needless to say, the King and Queen were very upset. They scoured the kingdom for the best doctors to treat the Prince in hopes of curing him. They tried medicines and prayers, they consulted the stars and filled the palace with various smoke; but nothing had any effect on the Prince. He continued flapping around the palace clucking indifferently to all these futile attempts on his behalf.

When all seemed lost, a wise old man appeared at the palace gate. He was provided an audience with the King. "Your Majesty," he said, "I can cure the Prince." The King looked hopefully at the old man but was perplexed. "Where are your medicines, your books, your instruments?" "I have my own ways," said the wise man. "Give me seven days, during which time I must be allowed the freedom to act as I see fit without interference, and I will set things right."

The King was skeptical, but he was desperate. So he agreed. "Good," said the wise man. "Now open all the doors and windows of the palace." "But it's very cold," protested the King. The wise man looked sadly at the King, and the King realized that he had already interfered. So, he ordered all the doors and windows to stand open. The wind whistled around the corners and billowed the drapes.

To the amazement of all, the wise man took off all his clothes and joined the Prince under the table where he was pecking at corn. The Prince stared at the wise man for a very long time. Then he spoke, "Who are you?" "Why, you can clearly see that I am a chicken the same as you," replied the wise man, and he began pecking at corn on the floor. The Prince seemed to be pleased at having the company, so they pecked together for a while.

But as the day wore on, they both began to shiver from the cold. Suddenly, the wise man reached for his clothes and put them on. The Prince was astounded! "Why are you wearing clothes?" He exclaimed, "You're a chicken!" The wise man calmly replied, "Where is it written that a chicken can't wear clothes? Just because you're wearing clothes doesn't make you less of a chicken." And he returned to a small pile of corn by the table leg. The Prince sat and thought for a long time. Then he retrieved his clothes, put them on, and rejoined the wise man on the floor.

The following day when the corn was brought for the morning meal, the wise man asked the servant to place his corn on a golden plate. Whereupon, he got out from under the table and sat in a chair. The Prince couldn't believe his eyes. "What are you doing?" he cried. "You're a chicken! Why are you sitting at the table?" The wise man finished chewing a mouthful of corn and said, "Where is it written that a chicken can't sit at the table? Am I less of a chicken if I eat from a plate?" The Prince thought for a long time and then joined his friend at the table.

For the next several days things moved in this manner. The wise man would request silverware and begin to use it. He then asked that the diet be varied and was brought meat, fish, and all varieties of vegetables. Wine and dessert were next, along with cordials and an occasional cigar. In each instance, the Prince would question the validity of the dietary and behavioral changes. But he was always met with the same answer, "Am I less of a chicken if I . . ." As the week drew to a close, the wise man and the Prince moved from under the table and began sleeping in their beds. "Don't worry, my Prince, you can be a good chicken even sleeping on a bed." They engaged in philosophy. "Wait a minute," said the Prince. "Chickens don't have to think and they certainly don't debate the merits of a way of life. They just exist, being fed and cared for without any worries."

"You may be right," answered the wise man, "but on the other hand, it doesn't mean you can't be a good chicken if you engage in discussion. After all, you still know you're a chicken just the same."

The Prince thought this over, and before long he was engaging everyone in the palace in various discussions and debates.

On the seventh day a great feast was held to celebrate the Prince's recovery. The Prince sat at his place at the table and held lively conversations with those around him. At one point he even proposed a toast to his father and mother and to his new friend, the wise man.

Toward the end of the evening, the wise man approached the Prince to bid farewell. As he was about to leave, he said, "My friend, remember—chickens are fair game for the hunter. So always try to pretend you are a human prince. Act wisely and help others. Farewell."

From that day on the Prince walked, ate, and talked like the prince he was. And when in time he became a great King ruling over the entire kingdom, no one besides himself knew that he was still a chicken.

This is a book about influence. So, why I have I told you this story? The essence of all I have to say on the subject is contained in this little fable. It is attributed to a Rabbi Nachman in eastern Europe during the mid-1800s. Anecdotally, it is said that it was a favorite of Sigmund Freud, who saw in this story the precursor of psychoanalysis.

Our focus in this book is on how to apply influence behavior more effectively in the workplace. However, as with so many other things, being effective at influence is a life skill as well. Your ability to become more effective at moving others in directions you want them to go has more to do with focusing on what is going on inside of them than what is going on inside of you. Those people out there whom we need to help us accomplish our goals and tasks, to give us a larger measure of their time and effort, and to prioritize their busy lives to accommodate us closer to the top of the list, may not all be chickens. But if we look hard enough and discern who they are, we can get down to where they live.

Acknowledgments

I would like to thank my colleague at The Communication Project, Martha Mesiti, for her hours of patient reading, excellent advice, and editorial assistance in the preparation of this book.

As a special note, I would like to dedicate this book to the memory of Linder Chlarson, who died this year following a short illness. He was a friend, a colleague, and an extraordinarily talented man who has helped me prepare the manuscripts for three books, composed beautiful music, and was a main factor in the success of The Communication Project. He will be sorely missed by all who knew him.

Also, I am indebted to Eric Valentine of Quorum Books for his encouragement, his direct and correct criticism, and the support he provided for this project.

PART I

Understanding Influence

If influence is to be used effectively in the workplace, it stands to reason that we need a cogent understanding of what it is. Moreover, "being influential" has been part of human interaction since recorded time, so why is it such an important component of corporate success today? This part addresses those issues. Chapter 1—The Rise of Influence—identifies the forces and circumstances that have elevated influence as a primary interpersonal skill in today's organizations. Chapter 2—Power versus Influence—defines influence by comparing and contrasting it with power, and makes a case that it can be learned. Chapter 3—Influence Strategies—examines the research surrounding influence and discusses the various strategies that come into play when influence is the goal. Finally, Chapter 4—Influence Styles—engages the issue of style, and focuses on the different preferences and susceptibilities we all bring to an influencing situation.

CHAPTER 1

The Rise of Influence

It is the nature of books to be, somehow, unsprung from time. I am writing this now, but you are reading it much later. So, it is a common wish of authors of nonfiction that the world would stand still at least until the book appears in print. I am having that feeling as I read through the 1997 AMA Survey, *Corporate Job Creation, Job Elimination, and Downsizing*. By the time you read this, there will be a 1998 survey, and things may have changed. I'm betting they won't change substantially. I also believe that the issues we will be discussing here will be more in focus, even more acute, a year hence than they are now.

I must also confess to a feeling of disorientation. The AMA Survey opens with this statement: "Job elimination and downsizing dropped to their lowest levels of the '90s as major U.S. firms created twice as many jobs as they cut in the twelve months ending June 1997."[1] The business press in recent weeks carried stories about major downsizing by Phillip Morris, Kodak, Polaroid, Cabletron, several managed care organizations, and merging banks. AT&T announced the projected elimination of 19,000 jobs—15 percent of their workforce. Even if it appears that jobs are being created faster than they are being lost, the broad numbers don't tell the story.

For the first time since 1992 (the year I consider the watershed for downsizing), a majority of the jobs eliminated belonged to hourly workers as opposed to supervisory, middle management, or professional/

Table 1.1
Jobs Created (in percent)

Twelve months ending:	6/95	6/96	6/97
Hourly (nonexempt)	50.3	59.8	62.3
Supervisory	9.0	8.2	7.6
Middle Management	9.3	7.1	8.6
Professional/Technical	31.5	24.9	21.6

Source: Corporate Job Creation, Job Elimination, and Downsizing: Summary of Key Findings. American Management Association Survey (New York, 1997), 2.

technical. When expressed in statistical terms, it appears that the trend for eliminating management and supervisory positions is slowing.

Table 1.1 shows that of the new jobs created in 1997, 16.2 percent fell in the management and supervisory categories. This sounds like good news for managers, but . . . Of the jobs eliminated in 1997 (Table 1.2), 31.7 percent came from the management and supervisory categories. That's still a loss of 15.5 percent from ranks of managers and supervisors who have already been severely depleted in previous years.

GETTING THINGS DONE

I have been tracking and studying employment trends and employee attitudes for the last decade, primarily because of my interest in the survivor populations—the workers who are left behind when the downsizing is over.[2] One thing comes through loud and clear—managers and supervisors are continually called upon to do more with less support staff and are taking on more responsibility—often with less authority. This erosion of authority, that has been the inevitable result of the continuing flattening of the traditional hierarchical organizational model, is the medium in which the need for influence as a palpable skill germinates. This need is then fed and nurtured by ambiguity, change, and insecurity, and grows to be the top leadership and survival skill required of today's managers.

It would seem to be a reasonable assumption that downsizing has ushered in another cycle of centralization, but this is where some of the ambiguity I mentioned comes into play. For many organizations the pattern of centralization followed by decentralization has been consistent and predictable throughout their history. It is widely accepted at the cultural level of most organizations, and, until now, not viewed as a

Table 1.2
Jobs Eliminated (in percent)

Twelve months ending:	6/95	6/96	6/97
Hourly (nonexempt)	45.0	48.7	54.6
Supervisory	17.8	15.9	15.0
Middle Management	15.3	19.9	16.7
Professional/Technical	22.0	15.5	13.8

Source: *Corporate Job Creation, Job Elimination, and Downsizing: Summary of Key Findings.*
American Management Association Survey (New York, 1997), 2.

completely bad thing because it kept things interesting and created new opportunities. Centralization is introduced as a means to solve problems of coordination. However, as time passes, this tight command and control is seen as stifling creativity, innovation, and initiative. The antidote is decentralization, which prevails until the old problems reassert themselves.

Traditionally, these cycles tended to occur in ten-year spans.[3] However, with so many downsizings and mergers taking place, there is a need as well as an impulse to centralize at least portions of the organization.

Now, let's throw in the change factor. Unless you have been living in a cave, you are already aware of the rapidly accelerating changes that are occurring in every aspect of life. For organizations, the change factors are technology and globalization. Competition has increased exponentially since companies are no longer protected inside their geographic region. The need to respond to change quickly and effectively has forced organizations to consider alternate models like matrix and systems approaches that purport to be more sensitive to environmental changes and allow for rapid response to changing conditions.

The matrix option was first introduced in the 1970s. Stan Davis and Paul Lawrence, in their book *Matrix*, discussed what they called the simultaneous needs of freedom and order.[4] The choice between freedom and order correlated to the choice of decentralization or centralization. They devised a system that was supposed to contain the advantages of both options while minimizing the disadvantages of each. As anyone knows who has tried to work in a matrix organization, there is extraordinary complexity. It has been decried by some theorists as a failure because companies develop a management process that is slow, acrimonious, and costly.[5]

Systems approaches are more promising because they are inherently more attuned to the change factors in the environment. Some organizations like Harley Davidson have used the approach effectively. Harley has replaced the traditional pyramid organizational chart with three overlapping circles: a Create Demand Circle, a Produce Products Circle, and a Support Circle. In the center, where the three circles intersect, there is the Leadership and Strategy Council. Quoted in a recent *Fast Company*, Jeff Bleustein, President and COO (Chief Operations Officer), elaborates on the system.

> The idea, says Bleustein, is simple and democratic. "We're applying the concept of self-directed work teams used in the factories to the executive level. Most management concepts get tried out as far from the executive offices as possible," Bleustein says, "At Harley, we said, Let's try this right up at the senior management level."[6]

The emphasis is on teamwork and individual approaches to solving problems as they arise.

General systems theory presents the organization as a group of interdependent parts—like departments. These parts interact to adapt to ongoing changes in the environment. All the parts are dependent on one another, and any change in one will affect all the others. This combination of coordination, change, and adjustment creates "synergy"—a combination of "synthesis" and "energy."

These system processes are thought to be "nonsummative," which implies that the outputs of such an organization represent more accomplishment than the combination of the parts would suggest. Or, as Gary Kreps put it:

> The whole is equal to more than the sum of its parts. Or, by working together, members of an organizational system can do far more to achieve organizational goals than they can by working independently. This nonsummative nature of cooperative activities in organizations indicates . . . the importance of teamwork in organizational practice.[7]

So, in an effectively functioning systems approach, the assumption is that everyone concerned is working interactively as a team. More often than not, with notable exceptions like Harley, this is an illusion rather than a reality.

RATIONAL VS. RANDOM

Most of us would like to believe that we are "rational actors" when it comes to making choices and decisions. The traditional models of decision-making support and attempt to institutionalize this notion. Legions of corporate men and women have been trained (at great expense) to follow a rational path toward the best decision. A large segment of the training industry has devoted its time, energy, and resources to package and deliver decision-making, project management, and other rational actor-based programs under various titles. Each puts its unique spin on the same rational model described over sixty years ago by John Dewey called *The Reflective Thinking Sequence*.[8] An astute observer of human nature, Dewey described seven steps in the problem-solving and decision-making process:

1. State the Problem

The first step is to state the problem in clear and concise terms. Dewey suggested that, rather than a "statement," the problem should be stated as a question such as, "What can be done to increase market share?" or "How can we get the new product to market by January 1?" It is also important that the question not contain a stated or implied solution that limits the possible alternative choices. "How can we increase the size of the technical staff in order to get the new product to market by January 1?" By including the part about increasing the technical staff, the question contains an implied solution that will limit consideration to only that alternative.

2. Define Terms

Language is an imperfect tool. When we share the same language, we have common meanings for the words in that language. However, there is a range of meaning that is created by ambiguity. For example, in the phrase "increase market share," what do we mean by increase? Ten percent? Twenty percent? If more than one person is involved in the decision process, clarity of definition is critical. This factor, called "bypassing," creates serious problems for organizational decision-making, and is the root cause of much frustration at meetings.

3. Develop Criteria

This step is often missed, or is applied later in the process. In the rational decision-making model, however, measures of a good decision must be established first before potential solutions are put into play:

- Quality cannot be compromised.
- Costs must be kept at a minimum.
- Potential customers need to be part of the development process.
- The new product must integrate effectively with current products in the field.

4. Suggest Solutions

Using the criteria as drivers, a list of possible solutions is generated.

- Schedule periodic meetings to ensure that all parties involved in the product development have access to one another.
- Create a Gantt project planning and scheduling chart that outlines everyone's responsibilities and delivery dates and have each person sign off on their part.
- At logical stages in product development, involve key customers and focus groups to ensure that the prototypes are meeting the targeted needs.
- Involve the quality control people from the beginning of development.

5. Measure the Solutions Against the Criteria

At this point, see how the various solutions meet the standards you have previously set. In a less rigid approach, steps 4 and 5 work together. That is, as a solution is generated, it is applied against the criteria, rather than waiting for the whole list to be complete.

6. Select (or Construct) the Best Solution

If the criteria have been developed and applied effectively, the best solution or decision should emerge from the available list. Organizational solutions are usually complex, so the end result will most likely be the best combination of the available solutions to choose from.

7. Develop a Plan of Action

This is the implementation stage. It may also begin a new round of problem-solving, and a new sequence or set of sequences.

When this model is applied, such as in group problem-solving, it often yields excellent results. Rational actors are very much in play in the sourcing and purchasing arenas. Management consultants and purchasers who are engaged in trying to determine the best possible supply for the least possible cost employ RFPs (Request for Proposal) or RFQs (Request for Quotation). In this rational actor process the criteria are expressed as a matrix, which potential suppliers either fit or don't fit, as the case may be. In some cases the criteria are weighted so that it is actually possible to come up with a numerical score that will determine which potential supplier meets the criteria best. RFQs and RFPs work best when the criteria are wholly objective. For example, if you are purchasing nuts and bolts, you might specify that the product must be made of an alloy that contains specific amounts of different metals, that they be uniform within a specific tolerance, and that the range of cost per piece must fall within two numbers. However, in many cases where RFPs are currently being employed today, such as in the sourcing of travel agencies or training companies or recruitment, important criteria tend to be more subjective. Customer service issues, interpersonal skills, and cultural sensitivity do not lend themselves to the same kind of measurement as cost and size. So, while rational actor models may be effective for certain kinds of decisions in the organization, much of the decision-making that takes place does not occur within the boundaries of this imposed rationality. The assumption that organizations are made up of rational employees who collaborate with each other to make rational decisions simply doesn't stand up under examination.

As Charles Conrad points out in his case against rational actor models in organizational decision-making:

> But in order to use this system successfully, we must have (1) a complete list of potential options and weighted criteria, (2) accurate and complete information about the outcomes and probabilities, (3) knowledge of all options, outcomes, and probabilities at the same time and/or the ability to use the same estimates during each of a

series of decisions, and (4) sufficient time and computational skill. In the most simple life (and organizational) decision situations, these requirements may be met. In most of the choices we face, one or more of the requirements will be violated.[9]

We learn from our culture that choices are made based on goals; that we always act consistently with our beliefs; that we make choices based on an examination of the probable outcomes of various courses of action. However, something very different is happening much of the time.[10]

As the raconteur and folk singer Gamble Williams was fond of saying, "Life is what happens to you while you're making other plans." Neither our world or our organizations adhere to a rational model. Decisions are more often made intuitively, with a lack of complete information, and are highly influenced by the situation within which the decision needs to be made. Managers often find themselves searching for the expedient rather than the best solution. Time is of the essence. Priorities are re-arranged on a moment-by-moment basis. People become emotionally in-volved with the decisions they make. In today's workplace, more often than not, managers have too many decisions to make.

This takes us back to the fact that there are fewer managers to handle more work. Organizations are still segmented into departments, and each department has its own priorities. The effects of downsizing have actually increased the psychological and communication distance be-tween departments because there are fewer individuals to play liaison roles, coordinate activities between departments, and build relationships. In theory, the reengineered organization should have just the opposite effect. Employees are asked to abandon old ways of structuring jobs and levels, and are supposed to think of themselves as team members, re-sponsible for one of the key business processes, reporting to a team leader and responsible to each other.[11] In fact, what often happens is that managers continue to equate information with power and guard it jeal-ously, individual achievement still takes priority over team success, and, despite best efforts, the quality of communication and decision-making deteriorates.

GETTING THE COOPERATION YOU NEED

Organizations are political systems. The members of these political systems are subject to the demands of power and circumstance. The de-cisions that people make and the way they assign their priorities are motivated by political, interpersonal, and personal considerations. Managers find their increasing numbers of goals and responsibilities going through constant change. There are inconsistencies, lack of definition, and loss of focus. Instead of being rational, managers cultivate a set of preferred solutions. As Cohen, March, and Olson suggest, those solutions are not developed to solve problems. Each manager takes his or her preferred solutions and searches the organization for problems to which they can be applied. In this view, an organization is a collection of solutions looking for problems, issues, feelings, and decision situations in which they might be aired. Managers are decision-makers looking for work.[12]

The fact is, despite the randomness of the decision-making process in most organizations, good decisions are still being made. As early as 1938, Chester Barnard provided an alternative view of how managers make decisions. His conclusion was that most decisions were made on the basis of intuition, not through rational processes.[13] Subsequent research and anecdotal evidence confirm that Barnard's view of how managers make decisions is accurate and that intuitive decision-making is quite often very successful. A key factor in intuitive decision-making is experience. The lesson of experience is the ability to recognize recurring patterns. For example, when it comes to predicting the weather, we are all amateur meteorologists. We enter into the endeavor with a mixture of limited scientific knowledge, observation, and a great deal of wishful thinking. Despite our best efforts, we are often wrong, and the picnic gets rained on, and the car without its snow tires can't make it out of the driveway. On the other hand, a professional meteorologist spends most of his or her waking moments studying charts, looking at patterns, and relying on past experience in order to make predictions of future events. And despite what we may think about the accuracy of the professional's predictions when our ball game gets rained out on what was supposed to have been a clear day, they are significantly more accurate in their predictions over time than are we nonprofessionals.

When an experienced manager is confronted with a business problem, he or she reaches for experience, discerns a pattern, and compares the situation to similar situations encountered in the past. Very often the right solution is arrived at quickly and intuitively. The danger is that, in a rapidly changing environment, past experience—while similar to a current situation—might lead to an incorrect response because of unrecognized or unthought-through factors in the current problem situation.

There is one additional outcome besides being right in your decision-making intuition or being wrong because you haven't considered the factors correctly. You could make a decision based on your best understanding of the needs for a particular action and the demands placed on your department or area of responsibility to produce a decision. And that decision yields excellent results for you and yet is disastrous for the organization as a whole. Consider the following real-life scenario:

A senior vice president at a large financial services organization is responsible for providing support to the field sales staff for a large category of financial products. The job requires ensuring that the training materials reflect accurately the provisions of all the products, ensuring that all materials that are released to the field have been put through a compliance process, and developing assessment and feedback materials to ensure that everyone in the organization selling the product has certified that he or she has sufficient knowledge of the product. A major new product is coming on line, triggering the need for a major revision in the existing field guide, training, and assessment materials.

Working against tight deadlines, the senior vice president (let's call her Sally) rapidly assesses her options in order to meet the deadline. She soon discovers that it will be impossible to get the necessary materials produced in-house during the time allotted. Making a quick decision, she outsources the job to a recommended consultant with whom the organization has an established relationship.

A project plan is developed, time lines established, and work progresses. One section of material that needs to be included in the package has not yet been completed by the product developer in charge. Despite repeated inquiries by Sally, the completed material is not forthcoming and the product developer—having finished other things that were pending—promptly takes a week's vacation. Since the project plan calls for the delivery of all the necessary product guides and inserts to the printer by a particular date, Sally has her assistant place an order for these materials. The response is very rapid and the following day over seventy boxes of material arrive at the printers. However, the packing list reveals that the boxes contain, at least by name, some of the requested items and several that had not been requested. Sally investigates and discovers that some of the materials for the field guide are on back order, and that other materials have been updated by the sales and marketing group and the names have been changed, without input from or discussion with members of any other department.

Sally makes another rapid decision, pares the number of inserts down to a bare minimum, and—as luck would have it—finds a cache of the necessary brochures, which are immediately dispatched to the printer. She then begins to prepare an insert to inform the field force that the remaining materials can be accessed when they become ready. In the process of doing so she contacts sales and marketing, who are unable to give her a firm date for the delivery of the materials. However, they also inform her that the materials she is preparing to use (that is, the second set of materials currently residing with the printer) will be out of date within the next two days and will be replaced with something new.

The result: one seriously missed deadline.

The interesting thing is that, from the perspective of each person involved, each of them did the right thing. Sally, faced with tight deadlines, made what would be excellent decisions and, in fact, would have had the materials in the field as scheduled. Sales and marketing, charged with a different type of responsibility, had assessed the available materials and decided that some serious revisions were necessary. Of course neither Sally or the sales and marketing people had any idea what the other was doing. The product developer had other deadlines besides the one that Sally was presenting him with and, for whatever reason, decided not to re-prioritize in her favor. Well, it is easy enough to say that the organization—at least in this instance—has a communication problem. This is not so easily fixed, given the staffing levels and rapid response requirements of today's business environment.

PUTTING PEOPLE BEFORE TASK

One of the byproducts of a low-staff, high-responsibility environment is the tendency to develop the illusion of self-sufficiency. Perhaps more than ever before, today's managers are not self-sufficient. They need a great deal of support, cooperation, and good will from their managers, other managers in the organization at their level, and employees at all levels who are key players in helping them get their tasks accomplished. Today's manager has become increasingly task-oriented. In fact, task orientation may be one of the primary survival factors for managers in the downsizing environment. Managers with a task orientation are usually recognized as making a more tangible contribution to the organization than other managers whose skills and abilities lie more in the area of organizing, controlling, or directing others. The challenge for today's managers, despite all the pressures to the contrary, is to shift their focus away from task and more toward the people in the organization. More than ever before, it is imperative to develop an informal network within the organization that can be called on and relied upon to provide the necessary tactical and political support necessary to achieve the desired goals.

In theory, this result should be accomplished through an established formal channel of communication. According to Lee and Zwerman, horizontal communication in a formal sense serves several important organizational functions:

1. It facilitates task coordination by enabling organization members to establish effective interpersonal relationships for the development of implicit contracts.

2. It provides a means for sharing relevant organizational information among co-workers.

3. It is a formal communication channel for problem solving and conflict management among co-workers.

4. It enables organization co-workers to give one another mutual support.[14]

Even under the best of conditions, horizontal communication has been overlooked and under-utilized in organizational practice. Because a formal application of horizontal communication is lacking, the individual manager must now establish these horizontal lines of communication through informal networks. Perhaps the most important factor that will determine how successful a manager is in developing and utilizing an informal network is his or her ability to apply influence.

An informal network is a grouping of organization members who interact with each other in some sort of pattern. Rogers and Argawala-Rogers discuss three types of communication networks.

- *Total system networks* which map the patterns of communication throughout the entire organization.
- *Clique networks* which identify groups of individuals within the organization who communicate more exclusively with one another than with other organization members.

- *Personal networks* in which individuals often interact with another organizational member.[15]

For the application of influence, personal networks are our most important consideration. These can be of two types: *radial* and *interlocking*. A radial personal network occurs when an individual interacts with selected people in the organization who do not necessarily interact with each other. An interlocking personal network occurs when all members of the network interact. Interlocking personal networks require a great deal of contact, and the individuals involved are generally similar to one another in level, function, interests, and so forth. When people do not interact frequently, this relationship has been called "weak ties."[16]

According to the theory of weak ties, the information provided in a weak network is greater than the information provided in a strong network. That is, people who do not generally interact have more new information to provide one another than people who interact frequently. For the manager who wants to gain more control over his or her environment through exerting influence, it is important to exploit the weak tie theory. Establishing new communication relationships in the organization can provide a manager with a broader perspective on the organization and enable him or her to influence prioritizing on other decisions in their favor. Before you can identify and nurture the skills of influence, you first have to identify who needs to be influenced on your behalf. Begin with the question, "How good is my network?" The *Successful Manager's Handbook* provides an evaluation check list that includes the following questions that a manager needs to ask about his or her network:

- Do you have a clear idea of what you need from a network?
- Have you analyzed what you have to offer other members of the network (for instance, skills, knowledge, information, or influence)?
- Do your colleagues contact you frequently for advice or support?
- Do you make an effort to get together with colleagues on an informal but regular basis?
- Do you volunteer to sit on task forces or committees to get to know higher-level managers and peers from other functional areas?

- Have you established a good working relationship with at least one key member of each functional area on which you must rely to get things done?
- Do you periodically attend professional conferences and make contacts with other key people in your industry and other industries?
- Are you an active member of at least one professional association?
- Do you regularly attend company social events?

Answering "no" to most of these questions raises another question: "Why?" Are you new to the organization? Do you feel uncomfortable with the idea of networking? Are you unsure about how to get started? Do you just not have time?[17]

Part II of this book will suggest a series of strategies for building more effective networks as part of your overall influencing initiative. But, for now, let's agree that more effective communication is the underlying issue; that:

- Despite best efforts, many organizations are failing to provide the formal structures and support needed for this communication to be institutionalized effectively.
- There is rarely enough information available to make decisions on a strictly rational basis.
- Today's manager exists in a highly conflicted and ambiguous environment.
- This ambiguity, instead of causing managers to seek out more information, causes just the opposite reaction.

The research on information-seeking behavior shows that when situations are unimportant, little information is sought. When an issue becomes confusing or threatening, more information is gathered—but only to a point. Under conditions of high ambiguity or threat, information may actually be avoided because it creates more confusion and anxiety.[18]

So, how does today's executive get the work done? The answer becomes increasingly clear: by establishing and nurturing his or her informal networks, and by influencing others to provide the necessary support and responsiveness to achieve the ever-changing goals.

In the business climate that many of us live in today, it is probably

safer to assume that the kind of disconnects—lack of information, con-
flicting priorities, ambiguity—described above will occur unless actions
are taken on a regular and continuing basis to avoid them. Also, in the
face of the demands placed upon today's workers, and in particular today's managers, it is hard to refocus our attention away from the task
elements of our job toward the human dimension. Yet, thrivers in today's
environment are continually discovering that the difference between success and failure lies more with the human side of the equation than with
the substance of what they're working on.

What we're talking about here is relationship-building—not just when
relationships come into play, but as a proactive measure to forestall any
difficulties that might be encountered in the future, and to facilitate getting one's needs prioritized. The day-to-day pace of events, combined
with the increasing need for data, works against the relationship side of
the equation. We tend to see others as sources and repositories of information, rather than as people with needs and expectations not unlike
our own.

While the opportunities to build relationships within the organization
are generally open to all—particularly on an informal basis—some managers do it better than others. In some cases the success experienced in
building business relationships is the product of simply making the effort. While some managers are naturally more personable than others,
anyone can initiate specific attempts to become more approachable or
take a personal interest in the people who work with them, resulting in
better interpersonal dynamics.

Managers who are approachable receive more feed-back about what
is going on. This serves to eliminate those surprises that create major
problems, such as Sally's dilemma described above. The chairman of my
department at C.U.N.Y. had a simple device for drawing people in. He
kept a large bowl filled with interesting and colorfully wrapped candy
in his office. During the course of any given day, he would have contact
with nearly everyone on the department. I'm convinced that he became
chairman largely through this device. The bowl said, in effect, my door
is open—I have something for you that you will like. We can meet for
a moment informally. Of course, during these moments important information was often exchanged.

To be effective, today's manager needs to make a point of being seen
more frequently by people in the organization. In those cases where colleagues are at remote locations, special efforts need to be made to main-

tain lines of communication and contact. Regular blocks of time should be scheduled and devoted to this particular effort.

If you are ultimately successful in becoming more influential, it will be primarily as a result of your ability to demonstrate an interest in the personal as well as the work-related concerns of your colleagues. Showing a willingness to openly acknowledge their fears and anxieties will go a long way toward building trust and cooperation. Managers who are effective at enhancing personal relationships find time for informal chats, and are interested in their colleagues' families, hobbies, and goals.

Another key factor in enhancing interpersonal relations with co-workers is an ongoing demonstration on your part that you can and will maintain confidentiality about the concerns of others. My chairman, along with the candy, would ask questions about issues he had come to know were important to each person who came to the bowl. Also, people quickly realized that the candy device was a good way to get a brief audience in an impromptu manner. It worked both ways.

So, like the wise man in our little story, we act independently; we seek out relationships; we take the interpersonal risk to learn and understand how those around us see the world. We meet them on a human level; we interact with them in a manner that is both comfortable and understandable to them; we gain their trust and alliance and ultimately, we lead them in the direction that we want them to go.

NOTES

1. *Corporate Job Creation, Job Elimination, and Downsizing: Summary of Key Findings*, American Management Association Survey (New York, 1997), 1.

2. Marvin R. Gottlieb and Lori Conkling, *Managing the Workplace Survivors: Organizational Downsizing and the Commitment Gap* (Westport, CT: Quorum Books, 1995).

3. Robert G. Eccles and Nitin Nohria, *Beyond the Hype: Rediscovering the Essence of Management* (Boston: Harvard Business School Press, 1992).

4. Stanley M. Davis and Paul R. Lawrence, *Matrix* (Reading, MA: Addison-Wesley, 1977), xi.

5. Christopher A. Bartlett and Sumantra Ghoshal, *Managing Across Borders: The Transnational Solution* (Boston: Harvard Business School Press, 1989).

6. Gina Imperato, "Harley Shifts Gears," *Fast Company* (June–July 1997): 105.

7. Gary L. Kreps, *Organizational Communication: Theory and Practice* (New York: Longman, 1986), 100–101.

8. Joseph A. DeVito, *Human Communication: The Basic Course* (New York: HarperCollins, fifth ed., 1991), 270–271.

9. Charles Conrad, *Strategic Organizational Communication*, 3d ed. (Fort Worth: Harcourt Brace College Publishers, 1994), 305.

10. James March, "The Technology of Foolishness," in *Ambiguity and Choice in Organizations*, edited by James March and Johann Olson (Bergen: Universitetsforlaget, 1970).

11. Gottlieb and Conkling, *Survivors*, 74.

12. Michael Cohen, James March, and Johann Olson, "A Garbage-Can Model of Organizational Choice," *Administrative Science Quarterly* 17 (1972): 2.

13. Chester Barnard, *The Functions of the Executive* (Cambridge, MA: Harvard University Press, 1938).

14. M. B. Lee and W. L. Zwerman, "Developing a Facilitation System for Horizontal and Diagonal Communication in Organizations," *Personnel Journal* 54 (1975): 400–401, 407.

15. Everett Rogers and Rekha Argawala-Rogers, *Organizational Communication* (New York: Free Press, 1976).

16. W. Liu and R. Duff, "The Strength of Weak Ties," *Public Opinion Quarterly* 36 (1972): 361–366.

17. Brian L. Davis et al., *Successful Manager's Handbook: Development Suggestions for Today's Managers* (Minneapolis: Personnel Decisions, Inc., 1992).

18. Bart Victor and Richard Blackburn, "Determinants and Consequences of Task Uncertainty," *Journal of Management Studies* 18 (1987): 108–132.

CHAPTER 2

Power versus Influence

If the rabbit outsmarts the dog, he doesn't get to eat the dog. He just gets to keep being a rabbit.

Thomas Perry

A colleague of mine recently retired after nearly forty years of teaching. One of the courses he taught with regularity was Persuasion. He is fond of telling this story. It seems that during one class session when he was trying to introduce the concept of persuasion to the students, he posed the following scenario.

"Here's the situation. I decide I want to go to the movies, but I don't want to go alone. So, I take out a gun and I point it at you and say, 'I want you to go to the movies with me!' Now, what would you do?"

One young man raised his hand in the back of the room and when called upon he said, "Mr. Isaacson, I'll go to the movies with you. You don't have to point a gun at me, just tell me you're paying."

This simple story illustrates much of what differentiates influence from power. This act of differentiating influence from power is not something that most of us do. However, if we are to hone our skills at influencing, we had better identify which behaviors we are targeting.

It's no wonder that there is confusion between the two terms. Even the media tend to use them interchangeably. We constantly hear or read phrases like: America has a lot of influence because of power, while European nations have more influence than they think, even though their power is diminished. Without power, America probably wouldn't have influence, but despite having little power, Europeans have influence, and so on.

It is the similarities between power and influence that create much of the confusion:

- Both power and influence develop and are maintained through communication events.
- People in organizations can develop both power and influence by developing certain personal attributes such as expertise, interpersonal skills, and the ability to provide access to other people.

Morgan W. McCall, Jr. in his monograph *Power, Influence, and Authority: The Hazards of Carrying a Sword* handles the distinction by simply declaring them one and the same. He discusses the fact that power involves both possession and skills. Some theorists consider power as something that can only be known when it is applied. Others see it as existing within a person whether it is applied or not. Then he opens up a curious line of thinking about the word "power" itself.

Numerous authors have attempted to label various aspects of power with words like influence, force, control, authority, and so on. The subtle distinctions drawn are hard to distinguish and are inconsistently applied across authors. Much of this confusion arises . . . because "power" has no verb form. Some authors treat influence as the power verb; others mean something entirely different. In this chapter, *power and influence will be used interchangeably.*[1]

I believe I know what McCall is reaching for, but "power" does have a verb form. The fact is that when you look at both of these concepts behaviorally, they are very different one from the other. Let's look at power first, since it is more commonly understood—and felt.

WHERE POWER COMES FROM

For the purposes of this book, the discussion of power and its uses or abuses is confined to what happens in or pertains to organizations. That is not to say that many of the same situations and manifestations of power do not occur elsewhere. However, as part of an organization's sociology, power is acquired, shaped, and applied according to the norms of that organizational culture. If you are on the receiving end of someone else's application of power, you will tend to think of it as tangible. But if you are in the position of applying power you will usually find that it is very situational. That is, you may be powerful in one place (such as in the office) and not powerful in another (such as in the home). So power, or the lack of power, is associated with your position or role in a given context.

In hierarchical organizations, power is usually determined by a person's position in the hierarchy. Some positions, more than others, put you in line for controlling workflow or communication networks or for becoming involved with the kinds of problems that require power behavior and actions.

Being able to control the information that flows through formal communication networks is very powerful. This is particularly true in organizations where formal lines of authority are not clear and stable. When communication processes break down, and lines of authority become ambiguous or confused, power over the source and dispersion of information tends to become highly politicized.

Charles Conrad, in his book *Strategic Organizational Communication: Toward the Twenty-first Century*, argues however that power has come in for a bad rap. He claims that the word power is presumably associated with the abuse of same, the implication being that there is something about power that is inherently evil. He argues that the abuse of power stems from imbalances rather than from power itself.

To some extent, powerlessness is a bigger problem than having power, since we all need to have the feeling that we have some manner of control over our lives. If a person perceives that he or she is powerless, this often leads to feelings of depression and helplessness, as well as manifestations of physical illness. Power, used to good purposes, can be very beneficial. Have we not all of us, at one time, feeling oppressed with the vagaries, vicissitudes, and complications of democracy, wished for a good and benevolent king who would simply come in, make the right decisions, and get the job done—whatever the job might be—to the benefit of the common good?

Conrad further argues that discussions of power in organizations tend to focus only on the overt conscious level—what he calls the "surface structure of power"—such as threats, promises, negotiations, orders, coalitions, and gag rules. However, power—according to Conrad—functions on a second level that he calls the "hidden face of power."

> [T]he processes through which employees decide which issues to raise in public, what arguments to present, and which actors to oppose and which to support; in short, what battles to fight and how to fight them. For example, a wide range of important kinds of conflict, including racial and ethnic discrimination, legal and ethical violations, and sexual harassment, are never discussed in organizations, not because people are not concerned about the issues, but because the discussion of them is suppressed.[2]

Conrad does little, however, to help us distinguish between the concepts of power and influence. Although not consistent, he tends to see power as an action and influence as a result. He describes the nature of powerlessness in this way: "Those of us who believe that our actions affect many people and events in enduring ways [*sic*] more satisfied with ourselves and our lives—and are more productive—than people who do not believe that they have sufficient power to influence their surroundings."[3] I think what he was trying to say in that sentence, with the word left out, was: ". . . affect many people and events in enduring ways are more satisfied . . ."

Much the same as the dilettante who says, "I don't know much about art, but I know what I like," power is something difficult to classify, but something that we all recognize when it's present. There is much agreement that power is a social construct, and that it is gained through interaction—that is, the answer to the question, "If someone is powerful and alone in the forest, who gets pushed around?" The answer is, of course, no one.

Also, power is not inherent. People are given power by others, based on their interaction and the relationship they develop. French and Raven were among the first to classify power. They divided it into five categories:

1. *Legitimate power*—an individual is perceived as powerful because he or she holds a position of authority that is accepted by others.

2. *Coercive power*—an individual is perceived as powerful because he or she can control the type or degree of punishments that can be meted out to others.

3. *Reward power*—an individual is perceived as having power because he or she can control the rewards that other people can receive.

4. *Expert power*—an individual is perceived as powerful because he or she has some special knowledge or information that is not available to others, and that others need.

5. *Referent power*—an individual is perceived as being powerful because he or she is personally attractive to others to the degree that they wish to identify with this individual.[4]

French and Raven's classifications are probably as good as anyone's. However, as Kipnis, Schmidt, and Wilkinson point out, these classifications—as with most power classifications—are guided by anecdotal evidence or armchair speculation that have been organized into rational classifications.[5]

Even Raven has pointed out that the categories are apparently not stable, since they tend to overlap and, when the existing classifications are actually studied, it is found that people do not apply power in ways predicted by rational classification schemes.[6]

In one study in which college students were asked to write brief essays on the topic "How I Got My Way," it was found that many of the tactics described by these students were not covered in the pre-existing categories. For example, the use of expert power was not only infrequently employed, it was not even mentioned by the students.[7]

INFORMAL POWER

In organizational life, controlling access to relevant information—and a willingness to barter that information—is a very powerful position. People who do not have formal, hierarchical power within the organization can gain power by gathering key information and disseminating it willfully in the pursuit of power. Often this is done through informal, rather than formal, communication channels. One interesting point about these informal leaders is that they wield a great deal of power within organizations, yet—strangely enough—they are usually not recognized by the individuals entrenched in the formal power structure of the organization as being either legitimate or powerful. The information that these informal leaders purvey, and build their power base upon, is generally information about the organization and not about the work of the organization.

The ambiguity rampant in today's organizations provides fertile ground for the development of these informal leaders. Many workers today will tell you that if it weren't for the "grapevine," they would never have any idea what was actually going on in the company.

It also is apparent that all attempts to rid the organization of these informal networks have the reverse effect. Restricting informal information flow seems to cause an increase in the very ambiguities that require the organization's members to seek out relevant information through informal channels.[8] In fact, we will discover as we move forward in our exploration of influencing skill, one of the primary vehicles for exerting influence is these informal networks.

Securing power, or influence for that matter, requires that you have a complete understanding of your own organization and your position in it. It is a paradox that most people are more powerful than they think. Taking an inventory of what your resources, abilities, and connections are in an organization is the first step toward assessing what, if any, power you actually have.

In sum, when most people experience power, they think of it in one of the following five categories:

Legitimate power. This is the ability to get others to do what you want because of the position that you hold. In many situations this sort of power comes from the title alone. Annoying as it may be, we generally sit and accept our fate when the police officer, often half our age, writes out that ticket for our not having stopped completely at the stop sign. We pull over in traffic when we hear the fire engines coming. We take our medicine as the doctor prescribes. And we do all these things because we operate on the basic assumption that they know what they're doing.

Coercive power. Anyone who has spent some time in corporate life understands that there are many times we have to take actions because the boss tells us to—not out of any respect for the judgment being applied but because if we don't do as we're told, the consequences would be unpleasant.

Reward power. Conversely, the ability to provide rewards and benefits gives a person a significant amount of power. Rewards can range from promotions to social acceptance to actual material gain, or the providing of physical comfort or pleasure.

Expert power. Anyone who has ever had to call a help desk for a solution to a hardware or software problem knows very clearly how much power the experts have. In situations where there is danger or where complex decisions need to be made, we will most often defer to the people who have the greatest measure of appropriate knowledge and experience.

Referent power. This type of power comes from an individual's attractiveness and social connections. That is, a person becomes powerful because others want to associate with him or her because of the resulting rise in status. In other cases, this power comes from the respect that we afford others for certain types of achievements or, in some cultures, for having reached the appropriate age.

In each of these circumstances, whether the power comes from a legitimate source, is coercive, provides rewards, demonstrates expertise, or exudes attractiveness and respect, there is something in the interpersonal dynamic that is inherent to the individual or to the situation and is readily understood and/or felt by all of the parties involved.

This is not true about influence. Actually, most interpersonal encounters, both inside of organizations and elsewhere, are so extraordinarily complex in the levels of awareness and unawareness that accompany such events that to try to isolate instances of this very common human behavioral interaction as being either purely powerful or purely influential is an exercise in futility. The reason why most people, including those who write about power and influence, have so much difficulty separating the two terms is that they are very often experienced simultaneously. That is why it is easy to say, "So-and-so is powerful; therefore he has influence over me," or "The most powerful members of this committee will most certainly influence the outcome." In these constructs, power becomes an instrument of influence—but I maintain that it is not the same thing.

Adler and Rodman provide an excellent example of a situation in which an individual possesses all five types of power to some degree, and yet has little or no influence on the actual outcome of the encounter:

> For instance, there are some times when the nominal leader—the person who is designated by title to direct the group's functioning—really has very little influence on a group. We remember

those happy days of junior high school when a certain substitute teacher took control (and we use that term loosely) of one civics class. She may have reigned, but she certainly didn't rule. Instead, a band of rowdy students, headed by two ringleaders with great referent power, ran the show: telling jokes, falling out of chairs, and finally escaping from the room through open windows. In the end, the dean's coercive power was the only way to put down the rebellion.[9]

Adler and Rodman go on to point out, in their discussion of leadership, that some nominal leaders don't really lead, and some superficially powerless members are in fact the real movers and shakers of the group. This is particularly evident when we experience effective leadership that is not power-based or centralized, but rather difuse and elusive. Some people are able to enlist the support of others by essentially sharing the leadership role. In this case, influence plays a key role.

CHARACTERISTICS OF INFLUENCE

To some degree, we all have power, as long as we retain our right to say "no" to the requests of others. In my definition, martyrs have power only at the moment they stand up against coercion and pay the big price. The sometimes extraordinary happenings that follow such an event are all, essentially, the result of influence.

The central issue of this book, and—from my view—a primary issue for organizations today, is how we gain compliance from others when power (either legitimate, coercive, rewarding, expert, or referent) is diminished or not accessible to us when we need to gain this compliance from others in order to succeed.

If we are to develop our ability to influence more effectively, we have to first see it as something separate, and very different, from power. Influence is not simply the result of the application of power. When we are in the grip of power, we are almost always aware of what is happening. The same is not necessarily true of influence. One of the best books on influence currently available is Robert B. Cialdini's *Influence: The Psychology of Persuasion*. Through research and selective anecdotal evidence, Cialdini presents very persuasive arguments about the unconscious works of influence. He uncovers the fact that human beings are programmed to react in certain ways, much as are other members of the animal kingdom. This programming operates much the same way in humans as it does with mother turkeys responding to the vocal sounds of their young chicks, or male animals marking and defending their territory. Cialdini calls these trigger features the "click, whirr" factors in influence.[10]

This is not to suggest that human beings react as mere automatons responding blindly to certain stimuli on a regular and consistent basis. However, it would be impossible for anyone to think through every aspect of life and react only in a purely rational and conscious manner. Trigger circumstances can be associated with certain value stereotypes. For example, there is a tendency to equate cost with quality. In many instances when this value is examined it is found to be true. The "trigger" effect occurs when a higher cost is placed on something that is not of higher quality. There is a tendency to respond to the item as if it were. It costs more, therefore it must be better.

There is a story told as a cautionary tale by country storytellers:

It seems that a truck pulling a horse trailer stopped in front of a general store. Everyone who saw the rig could tell that the owner was a person of wealth. The truck was shiny and new. The horse trailer well appointed and very roomy for the transportation of one horse. In the trailer was a very fine looking mare that showed the lines of a thoroughbred.

The man entered the store and moved directly to the stove to warm himself. It was a very cold day in December. He began looking about on the shelves. The owner of the store greeted him and asked him what he needed. The man said, "I need your best horse blanket for my race horse in the trailer." The store owner assured him that his search had ended and went into the back room to select a blanket from the pile—a blue plaid. When he brought it in and put it on the counter, the man looked dubiously at it and said, "Are you sure this is your best blanket? How much is it?" "$14.95," said the store owner, "All wool." The man moved closer to the store owner and adopted a confidential tone. "Maybe I didn't make myself clear," he said. "Do you see that horse in the trailer out there?" The store owner looked through the window. The man went on, "That horse cost me $5,000. Do you expect me to put a $14.95 blanket on her? I said your best blanket, if you don't mind." The store owner showed a look of realization. "I'm sorry sir. You are correct.

I'm sure I have just the item for your liking." He returned to the back room and took another $14.95 blanket from the pile—a red plaid this time—and brought it to the counter. "This is our very best blanket," he said, "I didn't show it to you the first time because it costs $100." "That's more like it," said the man as he reached for his wallet with one hand while he felt the quality of the wool with his other.

We need shortcuts in order to deal with the complex stimuli in our environment. We have to use stereotypes or other value judgements in order to classify things according to a few key features. When these features are present, we respond in predictable ways. Possessing an understanding of the response triggers of another puts the influencer in a very good position to gain compliance. Several of the more generic triggers are discussed in the chapters making up Part II of this book.

When provided with the challenge, most people can effectively differentiate between influence and power. Based on data collected from several hundred participants in workshops on influencing and related subjects, The Communication Project, Inc. has compiled a list of attributes that are associated with people perceived as being influential.

Influential people are perceived as:

- being supportive of the efforts of others, often without solicitation
- making an effort to be truly helpful, on both the personal and professional level
- being willing to share power, success, and recognition with others
- being trustworthy in the area of maintaining confidences, making efforts to achieve consensus on important issues
- being willing to collaborate with others to achieve a common goal
- effectively bringing people and ideas together
- being open, approachable, and accepting of constructive criticism
- being effective in establishing ground rules that everyone can relate to
- having an openness to change and a willingness to try new ideas
- engaging in as thorough an examination of available alternatives as possible before making decisions

- presenting a consistent picture of self—both personally and with regard to business issues
- providing help and direction in the area of clarifying roles, tasks, and responsibilities
- serving as a model for the behavior they espouse in others
- treating differences of opinion as an opportunity to enhance a solution, rather than as a roadblock
- leading from a position of competence rather than of status
- presenting themselves as non-defensive
- listening to others effectively and being responsive
- willing to make decisions and keep commitments
- being accessible

While many of these descriptions relate directly to personality factors that may be difficult to alter in a significant way, many others will yield to efforts to change and improve.

So, in some way, power and influence are contextual. The same person may be powerful in one situation and influential in another. A young man who had just finished his tour of duty and had been released from the Air Force entered the fall semester of a Western university. One morning, he was ten minutes late for his nine o'clock class. The professor, knowing the young man was on the GI Bill, bawled him out in front of the class. "When you were in the military and came in late like this," the professor said, "what did they say to you?" "When I came in late," the student said, "they just stood up, saluted, and said, 'How are you this morning, Colonel, sir?'"

NOTES

1. Italics are mine. Morgan W. McCall, Jr., *Power, Influence, and Authority: The Hazards of Carrying a Sword*, Technical Report Number 10 (Greensboro, NC: Center for Creative Leadership, 1978), 4.

2. Charles Conrad, *Strategic Organizational Communication: Toward the Twenty-First Century*, 3d ed. (Fort Worth: Harcourt Brace College Publishers, 1994), 268.

3. Ibid.

4. John R. French and Bertram Raven, "The Bases of Social Power," in *Studies in Social Power*, edited by D. Kartwright (Ann Arbor: University of Michigan Press, 1959).

5. David Kipnis, Stuart M. Schmidt, and Ian Wilkinson, "Intraorganizational

Influence Tactics: Explorations in Getting One's Way," *Journal of Applied Psychology* 65, no. 4 (1980): 440.

6. B. H. Raven, "The Comparative Analysis of Power and Influence," in *Perspective on Social Power*, edited by J. T. Tedeschi (Chicago: Aldine, 1974).

7. Kipnis, Schmidt, and Wilkinson, "Intraorganizational Influence," 440–441.

8. Gary L. Kreps, *Organizational Communication: Theory and Practice* (New York: Longman, 1986), 204.

9. Ronald B. Adler and George Rodman, *Understanding Human Communication*, 3d ed. (New York: Holt, Rinehart and Winston, 1988), 251.

10. Robert B. Cialdini, *Influence: The Psychology of Persuasion*, rev. ed. (New York: Quill, William Morrow, 1984), 3–5.

CHAPTER 3

Influence Strategies

On the whole, there is very little research conducted specifically on influence as a separate entity. Perhaps that is the result of the continual confusion of influence with power, or the fact that it is an elusive construct. However, some very promising research was conducted by David Kipnis and Stuart M. Schmidt from Temple University and Ian Wilkinson from the University of New South Wales.

What is particularly pertinent about this research is that it focuses on influence as a behavior in the workplace. While Maslow, Herzberg, and others have studied influence from the perspective of motivation, the Kipnis, Schmidt, and Wilkinson studies go beyond the motivational goal of improving subordinate productivity and morale. While several theorists, including Israeli, Schein, Etzioni, and French and Raven, have attempted to organize and classify various types of influence strategies (most often called "power tactics"), there have always been problems in carrying forward research in these classifications.

The problem is that they tend to overlap each other. Also, it appears that when acts of influence are actually studied, it is found that people do not exercise influence in ways predicted by rational classification schemes. One study that pointed that out was conducted by Goodchild, Quadrado, and Raven, in which college students were asked to write brief essays on the subject: "How I Got My Way." It was found that many of the influence tactics described by these students could not be

Table 3.1
Reasons for Exercising Influence, by Target Status (in percentages)

Reasons	Target Status			
	Boss (62)	Co-worker (49)	Subordinate (54)	Total (165)
Obtain assistance on own job	3	48	9	18
Get others to do their jobs	13	23	46	27
Obtain personal benefits	58	10	0	25
Initiate change in work	26	15	28	23
Improve target's job performance	0	4	17	7

Note: Numbers in parentheses are Ns.

Source: David Kipnis, Stuart M. Schmidt, and Ian Wilkinson, "Intraorganizational Influence Tactics: Explorations in Getting One's Way," Journal of Applied Psychology 65, no. 4 (1980), 441.

classified into pre-existing categories. Several tactics thought to be basic when classifying influence, such as the use of expert power, were not even mentioned by the students.

Feeling the need to enhance the existing classifications, or re-classify influencing behaviors, Kipnis, Schmidt, and Wilkinson focused their study on managers who—like most of us in the workplace today—faced the problem of influencing their bosses, co-workers, and subordinates. An assignment to write about an incident in their work environment when they actually succeeded in getting their boss, co-worker, or subordinate to do something they wanted, was given to 165 managers who were employed as engineers, technicians, and professionals. The essays were then collected and sorted in terms of the goal sought from the target person. The categories that emerged were easily recognizable. There were five in all:

1. assistance with one's own job
2. getting others to do their job
3. obtaining benefits (such as salary increase, promotion, or improved work schedule)
4. initiating change
5. improving performance

The goals that were selected were related directly to the target's job status. Table 3.1 is reproduced from the study.

Respondents sought mostly self-interest goals from their superiors, and the primary goal sought from co-workers was assistance with the respondents' own jobs. This speaks to the heart of the matter with which we are most concerned in this book. It is interesting, although not a surprise, that the most prevalent reason for influencing subordinates was to get them to do *their* jobs. The goal of initiating change was sought both from bosses and from subordinates, in almost equal proportion. However, the changes sought from superiors focused on job-related organizational changes, such as launching a new accounting procedure or starting a special project; but from subordinates the changes sought dealt with job performance, such as changes in the way a job should be done, or the manner of working in the organization.

The essays were combed through a second time, and a total of 370 influence tactics was extracted from the 165 respondents. These tactics were then sorted into fourteen categories, reported in Table 3.2.

As Table 3.2 shows, the categories ranged from the use of administrative sanctions and personal threats through the use of logic and rational discussions to clandestine dependency appeal and ingratiating tactics.

The influencing tactics used by the respondents varied with the goal. When the goal was self-interest, the most frequently reported tactics were self-presentation and personal negative actions. When the goal was to initiate change, the most frequently reported tactics were the use of logic and rational discussions. When the goal was to improve a target's performance, respondents reported using administrative tactics, training, and simply demanding compliance. But when the goal was to get others to do the respondent's own work, the most frequently reported tactic was the use of requests.

The kinds of influence tactics used by respondents were related to the perceived power of the target person. For example, individuals used more self-presentation, supporting data, and coalitions with others when attempting to influence their superiors. However, when it came to influencing subordinates, they more often used clandestine tactics, administrative sanctions, training, demanding, and explaining.

Notably, only one tactic was significantly associated with influencing co-workers, and that was the tactic of requesting help. However, the tactics of exchange, requests, or rewards were also associated with influencing co-workers, even though they did not achieve statistical significance.

Another finding pointed to the need for and use of a personal network. When the target people, whether bosses or co-workers, resisted the initial

Table 3.2
Classification of Influence Tactics by Category

Category/Tactic	Percent
Clandestine	8

Challenged the ability of the target
Lied to the target
Acted in a pseudo-democratic manner
Puffed up the importance of the job
Manipulated information
Made the target feel important
Cajoled the target
Showed understanding (pretended) of the target's problem

Personal negative actions   8

Fait accompli/went ahead on own
Chastised the target
Became a nuisance
Slowed down on the job
Held personal confrontation with target
Threatened withdrawal of help
Expressed anger
Threatened to leave job
Blocked target's actions
Ignored target

Administrative negative actions   3

Filed a report with supervisor
Sent target to superior for conference
Gave unsatisfactory performance evaluations
Gave no salary increase
Threatened with unsatisfactory performance ratings
Threatened job security
Threatened loss of promotion

Exchange   8

Contributed in exchange for compliance
Compromised
Offered to make sacrifice
Offered help to get the job done
Invoked past favors

Persistence   7

Repeated reminders
Argued
Repeated previous actions
Surveillance

Training   6
    Explained how it was to be done
    Showed how to do it

Reward   2
    Verbal reinforcement
    Salary raise
    Gave benefits

Self-presentation   5
    Demonstrated competence
    Performed well, then asked
    Waited until target was in the right mood
    Was humble
    Was friendly

Direct request   10

Weak ask   6
    Showed dependency
    Weak request

Demand   7
    Invoked rules
    Ordered
    Convened formal conference
    Set time deadline
    Told target that it must be done as I said or better proposed

Explained rationale for request   17

Gathered supporting data   6

Coalitions   7
    Obtained support from co-workers
    Obtained support informally from superiors
    Obtained support from subordinates
    Threatened to notify an outside agency
    Made formal appeals to higher levels

Source: David Kipnis, Stuart M. Schmidt, and Ian Wilkinson, "Intraorganizational Influence Tactics: Explorations in Getting One's Way," *Journal of Applied Psychology* 65, no. 4 (1980), 442.

attempts at influence, the respondents reported an increase of coalitions with fellow employees.

The researchers concluded that tactics were selected based on the perceived power of the target person and the degree of resistance. Administrative sanctions and personal negative actions are more likely to be used when the target is a subordinate who is actively resisting the request of the manager, and when the reasons for exercising influence are based on the respondent's role in the organization.

In a second study, Kipnis, Schmidt, and Wilkinson attempted to go further in classifying influencing tactics based on the actual influence behaviors of organizational members. Targeting the same population, they developed a questionnaire with three forms. One asked respondents to describe how they influence their bosses; another asked how they influenced their co-workers; and the third asked how they influenced their subordinates. In each case, the respondents were asked to describe, on a five-point scale, how frequently during the past six months they had used each item listed in the questionnaire to influence the target person at work. In addition to describing how frequently each influence tactic was used, a separate scale presented respondents with five possible reasons for influencing the target person. These reasons were based on those found in the first study:

- have my boss (co-worker or subordinate) assist me on my job or do some of my work

- assign work to my boss (co-worker or subordinate) or tell him or her what to do

- have my boss (co-worker or subordinate) give me benefits such as raises, better hours of work, time off, better job assignments, and so on

- have my boss (co-worker or subordinate) do his or her own work, or do what they are supposed to do

- have my boss (co-worker or subordinate) accept my ideas for changes—for example, to accept a new way of doing the work more efficiently, or a new program or project

For each of the five reasons, the respondents were asked to rate—on a five-point scale ranging from "very often" (5) to "never" (1)—how frequently each reason had been the cause of their trying to influence the target person to do something.

As with the first study, the reasons for exercising influence varied with whether the target person was a superior, co-worker, or subordinate. Using a factor analysis of the entire sample, the researchers isolated what they called "six interpretable factors." That is, the fifty-eight items on the questionnaire grouped themselves into six categories, which were:

Factor One—Assertiveness

Factor Two—Ingratiation

Factor Three—Rationality

Factor Four—Sanctions

Factor Five—Exchange of Benefits

Factor Six—Upward Appeal

According to the analysis, Assertiveness emerged as a dimension of influence at all target status levels. That is, it was used regardless of whether the person being targeted was a superior, a co-worker, or a subordinate. However, Assertiveness (and Sanctions) were used more often to influence subordinates than co-workers or superiors.

Ingratiation also emerged as a dimension of influence for all of the target groups, and included as part of this factor were the non-intrusive tactics, such as acting humble and making the other person feel important.

Rationality, which included such tactics as writing a detailed plan and explaining the reasons for the request, was also employed with each of the target status levels. However, when the tactic was directed toward subordinates, there were additional items involving groups that also came into play.

The Sanctions factor included those tactics that incorporated the use of administrative sanctions, including preventing salary increases and threatening job security.

The Exchange of Benefits factor included such tactics as offering an exchange and offering to make personal sacrifices.

Upward Appeal also loaded heavily in favor of those tactics that were directed toward superiors. The tactics grouped in this category were those that called for additional pressure for conformity by invoking the influence of higher levels in the organization, such as making a formal appeal to higher levels and obtaining the informal support of higher-ups.

The overall findings suggest that, as the status of the target person increased, respondents placed more reliance on Rationality tactics. Assertive tactics and Sanctions were used more often to influence subordinates than co-workers or superiors. The tactics of Ingratiation, Exchange of Benefits, and Upward Appeal were used with equal frequency among subordinates and co-workers, but significantly less often when attempting to influence superiors. Finally, respondents reported that they used Rationality tactics more frequently to convince superiors than co-workers or subordinates.

Looking at the data another way, the researchers also concluded that respondents who were trying to get personal assistance from others used Ingratiation tactics with some frequency, while respondents who frequently assigned work to others used Assertiveness, and respondents who frequently tried to improve a person's performance used Assertiveness and Rationality tactics. Rationality also appears to be most often employed as a tactic when trying to convince others to accept new ideas.

A person's own level in the organization seems to determine the type of tactics he or she will use. Respondents with higher job status used more Rationality and Assertiveness when influencing both their subordinates and their superiors. They also used Sanctions more frequently and sought aid from their superiors less frequently when influencing their subordinates.

It was also interesting that the presence of unions was associated with the use of certain tactics. If the organization had a union, respondents used more Ingratiation to influence subordinates, and avoided Assertiveness when influencing co-workers.

There were no significant relationships associated with the sex of the respondents, or the sex of the respondents' bosses in terms of the frequency of use of any of the strategies. The researchers concluded that men and women chose similar tactics when attempting to get their way.

REFINING THE CATEGORIES OF INFLUENCE STRATEGIES

The Kipnis, Schmidt, and Wilkinson studies, along with the earlier studies done in the 1970s (Israeli, Schein, French and Raven, etc.), went a long way in defining the types of strategy used when people found themselves in compliance-gaining situations.

Another part of the study attempted to categorize influencing behaviors using an inductive approach. Subjects were asked to examine ten persuasive situations, and to rate each of these situations in terms of their believability, their importance, the reasonableness of the requested compliance, and the degree to which the problem in the persuasive situation violated social norms. The subjects were also required to select three persuasive situations that they identified closely with, and to construct a persuasive message for each of the three situations. Finally, they were asked to write an essay on "How I Get Others to Do What I Want Them to Do." All of the essays were then subjected to content analysis. The researchers reported that there were four significant properties of compliance-gaining strategies that determined the approach a person would use when applying influence:

- Whether the persuader's intent is revealed in the message
- Whether the persuader is manipulating some reward or punishment
- Whether the persuader controls that reward or punishment
- Whether a rationale for the persuader's desired compliance is given

Table 3.3 lists fourteen categories of influencing behaviors, along with the names, definitions, and examples of the strategies.

Schenck-Hamlin et al. further divide the strategies into four basic types.

1. Sanction Strategies
2. Altruism Strategies
3. Argument Strategies
4. Circumvention Strategies

Each of these categories is representative of a particular persuader's intent. That is, whether the persuader is manipulating some reward or punishment, whether the persuader controls that reward or punishment, and whether a rationale for the persuader's desire for compliance is given. These categories and the description of the characteristics associated with the fourteen behaviors described in Table 3.3 are useful as a springboard to a model for examining and preparing appropriate behaviors for a variety of influence situations.

Since the studies are looking at groups of people, it is useful to examine and understand how an individual might relate to influencing situations from his or her perspective of what kind of compliance behavior is necessary. From that perspective there are essentially three ways in which an individual can exert influence on another individual or a group: intrinsic influencers, extrinsic influencers, and strategic influencers. Figure 3.1 presents a summary of these factors and their relationship to one another.

Table 3.3
Definitions of the Strategies

Sanction Strategies

Reward Appeals

Rewards are controlled by the actor.

1	**Ingratiation**	Actor's proffered goods, sentiments, or services precede the request for compliance. They range from subtle verbal or nonverbal positive reinforcement to more blatant formulas of "apple-polishing" or "brown-nosing." Manipulations in behavior include gift-giving, supportive listening, love and affection, or favor-doing. Form: Present reward from actor implies compliance.
2	**Promise**	Actor's proffered goods, sentiments, or services are promised the target in exchange for compliance. This may include a bribe or trade. A variant is compromise, in which gains and losses are perceived in relative terms, so that both actor and target give in order to receive. Sometimes compromise is called trading-off, log-rolling, or finding a "middle-of-the-road" solution. Form: Compliance implies future reward from actor.
3	**Debt**	Actor recalls obligations owed him or her as a way of inducing the target to comply. Past debts may be as tangible as favors or loans, or as general as the catchall "After all I've done for you . . ." Form: Past reward from actor implies compliance.

Rewards are controlled by the target.

4	**Esteem**	Target's compliance will result in automatic increase of self-worth. Actor's appeal promises this increase in areas of target's power, success, status, moral/ethical standing, attention and affection of others, competence, ability to handle failure and uncertainty well, and/or attempts to aspire. "Everyone loves a winner" is the fundamental basis for appeal. "Just think how good you will feel if you would do this." Form: Compliance implies future reward because of target's action.

Rewards are controlled by circumstance.

5	**Allurement**	Target's reward arises from persons or conditions other than the actor. The target's compliance could result in a *circumstance* in which other people become satisfied, pleased, or happy. These positive attitudes will be beneficial to the target. "You'll always have their respect" is an example. Form: Compliance implies future reward because of the action of forces other than the actor or target.

Punishment Appeals

Punishments are controlled by the actor.

6 **Aversive stimulation** Actor continuously punishes target, making cessation contingent on compliance. Pouting, sulking, crying, acting angry, whining, "the silent treatment," and ridicule would all be examples of aversive stimulation. Form: Non-compliance implies present punishment.

7 **Threat** Actor's proposed actions will have negative consequences for the target if he or she does not comply. Blackmailing or the suggestion of firing, violence, or breaking off a friendship would all be examples of threats. Form: Non-compliance implies future punishment.

Punishments are controlled by the target.

8 **Guilt** Target's failure to comply will result in automatic decrease of self-worth. Areas of inadequacy might include professional ineptness, social irresponsibility, or ethical/moral transgressions. Form: Non-compliance implies future punishment because of target's actions.

Punishments are controlled by circumstance.

9 **Warning** Target's punishment arises from persons or conditions other than the actor. The target's non-compliance could lead to a *circumstance* in which other people become embarrassed, offended, or hurt. Resulting negative attitudes from those people will have harmful consequences for the target. "You'll make the boss unhappy" and "What will the neighbors say?" are examples. Form: Non-compliance implies future punishment because of the action of forces other than the actor or target.

Altruism Strategies

10 **Altruism** Actor requests the target to engage in behavior designed to benefit the actor rather than the target. Asking the target for help is typical. Intensity of the appeal may be manipulated by making the target feel unselfish, generous, self-sacrificing, heroic, or helpful. "It would help me if you would do this," and "Do a favor for me," exemplify the direct approach of the altruistic strategy. Two variants are sympathy ("I am in big trouble, so help me.") and empathy ("You would ask for help if you were me.") Form: Comply for my sake.

Argument Strategies

Response is controlled by the Rationale, and Rationale is *not* revealed by the actor.

11 **Direct Request** The actor simply asks the target to comply. The motivation or inducement for complying is not provided by the actor, but must be inferred by the target. In some cases the

Table 3.3 continued

actor's message appears to offer as little influence as possible, so that the target is given the maximum latitude of choice. "If I were you, I would . . ." and "Why don't you think about . . ." are instances of direct request. In other cases the strategy takes on a form where the actor demands the target's compliance. Examples would be "I want you to do this" and "Do this." Form: You (might) comply.

Response is controlled by the Rationale, and Rationale is revealed by the actor.

12   **Explanation**   One of several reasons are advanced for believing or doing something. A reason may include the following: (1) credibility: "I know from experience." Form: The reason for complying is my trustworthiness, integrity, exemplary action or expertise; (2) reference to a value system: "It's in the best interests to . . ." Form: Since we value this, you should comply; (3) inference from empirical evidence: "Everything points to the logic of this step." Form: The reason for complying is based on the following evidence.

Response is controlled by the Rationale; situational context is revealed by the actor.

13   **Hinting**   Actor represents the situational context in such a way that the target is led to conclude the desired action or response. Rather than directly requesting the desired response, the actor might say, "It sure is hot in here," rather than directly asking the target to turn down the heat. Form: Given this context, target should infer desired response.

                              Circumvention Strategies

14   **Deceit**   Actor gains target's compliance by intentionally *misrepresenting* the characteristics or consequences of the desired response. "It's easy," when in fact it is neither simple nor easy. "By doing this, you'll be handsomely rewarded," but the actor does not have the ability to give that reward. Form: Given false rationale or reward, compliance is requested.

Source: Adapted from Richard L. Wiseman and William Schenck-Hamlin, "A Multidimensional Scaling Validation for an Inductively Derived Set of Compliance-Gaining Strategies," *Communication Monographs* 4 (1981), 257.

THE GOTTLIEB INFLUENCING MODEL

Intrinsic Influencers

The intrinsic influencers in the model are derived from the earlier research done by The Communication Project, Inc., where people were

Figure 3.1
The Gottlieb Influencing Model

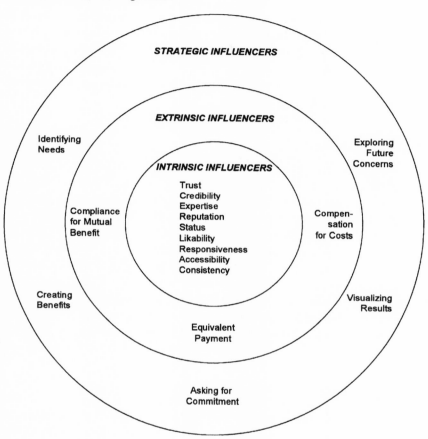

asked to name those qualities that an individual would possess whom they would perceive as influential (see Figure 3.1). Many of these intrinsic influencers such as trust, credibility, reputation, likability, responsiveness, accessibility, and consistency are clearly connected to the individual's ability to establish relationships with the people targeted for compliance behavior. Also, factors such as likability and responsiveness are directly related to personality variables and are often dictated by differences or similarities in style. The issue of style connections and disconnections is covered in Chapter 4. Other factors such as expertise, accessibility, and consistency are behaviors that can be cultivated by anyone regardless of personality type or style.

Intrinsic influencers, because of their connection with personality style and behaviors that others have observed over some period of time, are the most difficult to grasp conceptually and to translate into behavior. However, unless a high degree of intrinsic influencers are present in any compliance gaining situation, you as the persuader will not be successful. To put it another way, no matter how well you might do everything else, if the people from whom you are trying to gain compliance distrust you, you will not influence them.

Extrinsic Influencers

Extrinsic influencers are a group of behaviors that are external to the basic personality. Their effectiveness centers around a correct determination of what the individual targeted for compliance will be responsive to. Often that involves effectively presenting the things that will be mutually gained through compliance.

In other cases you may find yourself offering up compensation in the form of time or resources in exchange for compliance on the part of others. Another option is a direct trade-off such as, "If you do this for me, then I will do that for you." Extrinsic influencers involve the exchange of value between those who would influence and those whose compliance is sought. These exchanges of value are covered in detail in Chapter 6.

Strategic Influencers

Strategic influencers come into play during the actual presentation of the influencing message. There is a way of presenting your point of view that has impact and helps ensure that the targeted individual will be motivated toward compliance. Strategic influencers are particularly evident in selling situations and are discussed in detail in Chapter 7.

So, as we can see to this point, although not a great deal of research has been conducted on the subject of influence, as a separate entity, the several studies cited and discussed in this chapter all seem to converge on the same points. When people are pressed to examine and identify those factors within their own behavior that they would describe as influential, they are not only able to do so, but they are able to describe specific situations in which each is applied. We move on from here to issues of style and application grounded in the understanding that influence exists separate from power, can be learned and perfected, and is essential for managers in today's workforce.

CHAPTER 4

Influence Styles

Up to this point we have been discussing some key issues relating to the executive's ability to be influential. We have highlighted the need to develop and maintain informal networks, and have discussed the various strategies available for applying influence to meet objectives.

One additional factor which is very important, but often taken for granted, is personal style. Almost everyone is flexible to some degree with regard to the style that they can employ in a given situation. Style is a collection of personality traits that become manifest when one person attempts to interact with others.

How one develops his or her style profile goes well beyond the boundaries of this book. However, psychologists tell us that style is the relationship between a number of potential response factors in the personality, ranging from our need to be competitive, to be accommodating, to collaborate with others in certain circumstances, and in other circumstances to avoid issues that are unpleasant to us. Although our core self-concepts are relatively unshakeable and unchanging, in our moment-to-moment interactions with the world we are able to draw on various aspects of this mix of available responses to assure that what we are presenting to the world is appropriate for the given situation that we're in. However, it has been demonstrated through the use of testing instruments that most of us present a fairly consistent predominant style when interacting with others.

Several instruments are on the market for use by Human Resources professionals and Corporate Training personnel that are designed to help individuals discover their predominant styles. Myers Briggs and Wilson Learning Systems are two of the better-known purveyors of such materials, and many organizations have used these inventories as part of management development and other corporate leadership programs.

Another excellent and much less complex instrument is the *Thomas-Kilmann Conflict Mode Instrument* (TKI) published by Xicom in Tuxedo, New York. This instrument grew out of the work of Kenneth W. Thomas and Ralph H. Kilmann. It is designed to assess an individual's behavior in situations in which the concerns of two people seem to be incompatible. The TKI is a self-directed test using a series of thirty forced-choice questions pertaining to conflict situations. The individual selects the most appropriate answer from each pair and then tabulates and graphs their scores. This determines their primary and alternative styles of handling conflict. These are displayed across five "conflict-handling" modes as "competing," "collaborating," "compromising," "avoiding," and "accommodating." Since its original publication in 1974, over two million copies of the *Thomas-Kilmann Conflict Mode Instrument* have been printed. The instrument's original validity study was based on the responses of 339 practicing middle- and upper-level managers.

The branch of psychology most concerned with style issues is the psychology of individual differences, or ID psychology. The concern of ID psychologists is the study of things that distinguish one person from another. It focuses on those traits and characteristics which point to why everyone doesn't act the same. Sex, age, education, occupation, socioeconomic level, intelligence, and many other characteristics are the items studied by the ID psychologist.

One of the variables, of course, is personality, and—although elusive—it is the most potent one. Style, to some extent, can be seen as the outward manifestation of a specific personality. Because each person's personality is somewhat different, this helps explain why—from a style perspective—we tend to respond to situations in totally different ways. When personalities and the resulting prevailing styles of two or more individuals are in conflict, this can create stress and further affect, alter, or moderate the interactions between the people involved. It is possible that the effect may be to intensify the relationship, as in the old saying "opposites attract." On the other hand, such conflict is just as likely to weaken a relationship. These style conflicts can have a serious negative effect on the ability to influence.

There are innumerable style traits that hold the potential for both attraction and repulsion among individuals. All people have dimensions of personality that serve to increase, or decrease, the stress they experience in a particular situation compared to the stress someone without those same characteristics would experience. The type of person who is always punctual will inevitably experience greater amounts of frustration with regard to appointments than do people who are more casual about being on time. Moreover, such a person will have a tendency to react negatively on an interpersonal basis to people who do not value punctuality.

While style differences can be very powerful determinants of how people interact, and to what degree one has influence over the other, what we are talking about is a prevailing style. The same personality construct that provides for our differences also provides for our similarities. Any style inventory you select and administer to yourself will demonstrate that, while you have a prevailing style, you also contain within your basic personality some measure of the other available styles. Our prevailing style emerges in much the same way as other personality factors. When we are very young, for whatever reason, certain behaviors are rewarded while others are ignored or punished. So, over time, we learn that we are most successful using a particular mode of behavior when we interact with the world and others.

Periodically, circumstances cause us to reach inside ourselves for a style of behavior that differs from our usual choice. While this may produce a measure of discomfort, the fact is that most of us are capable of sustaining alternative styles for some period of time when it benefits us to do so. Where we get into trouble—and why this is so important in the area of influence—is that, unless we focus our attention on the need to reach for different styles in various kinds of interaction situations, we will automatically migrate to our prevailing style, which may or may not be appropriate for the given circumstance.

Jerome D. Frank in his classic work on psychotherapy called *Persuasion and Healing*, focuses on the relationship between style and influence and the problems that arise from the reciprocal nature of human transactions. When you interact with someone else with some degree of frequency over time, one person's behavior tends to "train" the other's to respond in such a way as to confirm your expectations. He cites as an example a paranoid patient who is convinced that everyone hates him, and who, because of his surly, suspicious manner, antagonizes other people who originally bore him no ill will. However, the resulting reaction he receives confirms the patient's belief that everyone dislikes him, intensifying his dislike-creating behavior. In this way, according to Frank, in the psychiatric construct, patients tend to get caught in "self-fulfilling prophecies," and their behavior is both self-perpetuating and self-defeating.

Frank then goes on to discuss more directly the forces of influence that practicing psychotherapists have available to them.

> To oversimplify vastly, the two major sources of interpersonal influence are individuals on whom a person feels dependent and those whom he perceives to be like himself. The former, first represented by his parents, later by teachers, bosses, and so on, gain their power through their direct control of his well-being. The sources of influence of the latter—his friends and colleagues—are not so apparent, but probably spring in part from the fact that their attitudes of acceptance or rejection determine his sense of group belonging.[1]

In his book *Influence: The Psychology of Persuasion*, Robert B. Cialdini supports this notion in another way. Following a discussion about the way in which attractive people in our society reap certain benefits, Cialdini talks about some of the other factors that enhance a person's influence.

One of those factors is similarity. "We like people who are similar to us. This fact seems to hold true whether the similarity is in the area of opinions, personality traits, background, or life-style. Consequently, those who wish to be liked in order to increase our compliance, can accomplish that purpose by appearing similar to us in any of a wide variety of ways."[2] Cialdini provides us with some examples, including the way we dress. He discusses one study, done in the early 1970s, when young people tended to dress either in "hippie" or "straight" fashion. The researchers running the experiment dressed either as hippies or straight people, and asked college students on campus for a dime to make a phone call. "When the experimenter was dressed in the same way as the student the request was granted in more than two thirds of the instances; but when the student and the requester were dissimilarly dressed, the dime was provided less than half the time."[3]

CATEGORIZING INFLUENCE STYLES

In order to be able to identify the various styles available to most of us, we first need to give them some names. If we examine the six factors discovered by Kipnis et al. in Chapter 3, we can develop a justification for categorizing influence styles into four subsets. Of the six (Assertiveness, Ingratiation, Rationality, Sanctions, Exchange of Benefits, and Upward Appeal), only the first four relate specifically to actions or behaviors generated exclusively by the person doing the influencing. That is, factors five and six, Exchange of Benefits and Upward Appeal, involve either some tangible or intangible exchange, or the solicitation of help and support from others in order to meet the influencing objectives. From a style perspective, we separate these behaviors into four types, which we will call Persuasion, Control, Trust, and Vision.

Persuasion

Individuals who exhibit a primary Persuasion style are fundamentally driven by logic, facts, opinions, and ideas. They are assertive in presenting their ideas, proposals, and suggestions, and they feel strongly that their approach to the way things should be done is the correct one. They are not afraid to take risks, and to present their ideas—even as a test of others' reactions. They are highly dependent on evidence and arguments from other sources, and tend to be quite good at finding these support materials. They are characterized by a persistent and energetic approach when persuading others.

Persuasives tend to be poor listeners, especially when the person speaking is in disagreement, yet they seem to be astute at picking out what they perceive as weaknesses in the other person's position. Rationality tends to overbalance emotion, and if a Persuasive has real power, he or she will tend to use that power to compel compliance.

When Persuasives are effective, it is usually the result of their being highly verbal and articulate, and of their willingness and ability to participate very actively in discussions and agreements. Persuasives differ from many of the rest of the styles in the sense that they actually enjoy being involved in arguments, and tend to be generally less conflict-averse than people not sharing that style. Persuasives tend to be found in law firms and legal departments of corporations. They often make excellent sales people, as well as management consultants.

Many people who migrate toward this style tend to depend too heavily on logic and fact to achieve influence. When Persuasion doesn't work, it is because people do not always approach situations or decisions logically and rationally. If a person has strong emotional feelings about an issue, reliance on a strong rational approach often results in higher levels of overt or covert resistance.

Persuasives tend to be at their best when they also have a measure of Trust in their style dimension. This tends to take some of the edge off the assertiveness and makes the person become more collaborative. They look for solutions to problems that are pragmatic and address the substantive or factual issues at hand, but also concern themselves with building relationships for a long-term payback. They will consult with and ask for the opinions of others who may be functional experts or staff members, and they are not afraid to share information with other people. Again, and at their best, Persuasives focus on overcoming a problem, not other people. They are adept at gaining commitment to integrative solutions, where the concerns of all parties can be reconciled.

On the other hand, if Persuasives have a high amount of Control behavior in their style, the result can be very difficult for others to deal with. This combination provides a very strong power orientation, and Persuasives with high Control rarely involve others in the planning process and feel that they must decide and carry out decisions on their own. To do otherwise would be a sign of weakness. There is also a tendency to over-control and dominate any conversations, and to set the communication rules. Interactions with this type of Persuasive will incorporate a style of pushing, demanding, and making flat assertions.

Control

Individuals with a prevailing style in the Control dimension base their actions and interactions on what they perceive as a solid belief system. On the positive side, Control people balance praise and criticism, and ensure that the people they interact with know exactly what they want, expect, or require of them. They set standards and tend to apply these standards consistently in judging behavior and performance. These are the detail people, and very often the ones to whom others turn to get work done.

The belief system that a Control person adheres to can derive from several different sources, such as policies and procedures; the rule book (as in the military); religious affiliation; accepted conventions of society; prejudice; or personal preferences based on previous experience.

A key problem for Control people is to make an effective distinction between assertiveness and aggressiveness. Being assertive means defending yourself appropriately by focusing your attention on the issues and arguments in question. Aggressiveness is another way of defending yourself; however, it generally results in direct attacks on the people posing the issues or arguments that are in contention.

Often it is more natural for Control people to overuse criticism at the expense of praise. We all know managers whose idea of providing praise for a job well done is to simply say, "Good job!" while, as soon as something doesn't go as planned, they provide very detailed criticism of everything that went wrong. To be effective in using Control, praise must also be used liberally and provided in a detailed way.

Individuals who have a prevailing Control style tend to be particularly effective when decisive, quick action which has the potential for unpopularity is required, as in an emergency situation. However, the long-term results and fallout from an application of heavy control may have extremely negative after-effects. Controls tend not to involve others in the planning process, and feel that they must decide and carry out decisions on their own. For some Control people, allowing others to participate in decision-making would be a sign of weakness. High Control people also tend to be surrounded by "yes" people, who have found it unwise to disagree. This tends to block off some potentially important information.

Trust

People with high Trust profiles have a need to involve (and sometimes over-involve) virtually everyone affected by the outcome of a situation. Their underlying way of interacting with the world depends on consensus. People with a high Trust style profile like working in teams and sharing ideas with others. They tend to be more willing to make concessions when confronted with conflict, and put their concern for their relationships ahead of winning or following an unpopular policy. Often they allow, and prefer, others to control the situation, and while this type of orientation will many times produce more creative solutions to problems, a group of high Trust people will spend an inordinate amount of time on relationship building. As managers, high Trust individuals depend on others to carry out plans and actions, and tend not to be as concerned with followup and supervision.

Unlike Persuasion and Control, which can be conceived as "push" strategies, Trust tends to pull people in as a means of influence. Effective Trust people are successful at making others feel that their resources are important to the task at hand, and that time and effort will be put forward in order to gain the valuable contributions of others. Trust people tend to promote an atmosphere of openness and non-defensiveness, and—as facilitators—often succeed in achieving a high level of participation. They are active listeners. They tend to be at ease showing their understanding and appreciation of others' contributions. They tend to be positive, and freely give over responsibility and authority to others working on their team.

As an influence style, Trust can be very effective in the right situations, since Trust people create a sense of openness and build relationships on a personal level that they can then draw on later when they need allies. Aside from being a powerful style of influence in and of itself, Trust works very effectively with the other styles, and should be cultivated as part of the behavior exhibited in situations requiring influence. One unique aspect of the Trust style is that it is reciprocal. In the process of applying the behaviors associated with Trust, a person leaves him- or herself open to be influenced.

On the negative side, they may take too long to get things done, and may over-emphasize the relationship at the expense of taking a stand or solving substantive problems. Also, there's a danger of Trust people personalizing any given situation. Some high Trust people have a strong need to be liked, and this makes them ideal targets for others who feel the need to tear them down or manipulate them. As managers, Trust people who are too accommodating may reinforce the perception of low authority and conviction. This can serve to undermine personal impact and credibility. It also diminishes the impact that any valid points that they might make would normally have.

Vision

People with high Vision profiles are focused on the future. While they are generally less concerned about relationships than Trust people, they depend on an emotional connection to have their influential impact. They tend to mobilize the energy and resources of others by tapping into their values, their hopes, their aspirations, needs, and wants.

High Vision people are adept at using altruistic approaches. They are effective at generating a sense of importance for being part of a group which shares a common purpose. They depend on being able to present ideas effectively; however, unlike Persuasives, their appeal is not primarily to the intellect. Effective Vision people have the ability to get others excited about the future as they perceive it. They have an enthusiasm that is infectious, and they are often charismatic. Unlike Trust people, they are not looking to build a consensus, or to share their ideas with others in the hope of arriving at a common solution or decision.

When a Vision person enters into an influence situation, he or she has already decided on what the outcome needs to be. The objective is to sell that idea to others to the extent that they will agree to work together to achieve the necessary common goal. On the negative side, Vision as an influencing style can create difficulties, on both a small and a large scale. On the world stage, we might say that people like Gandhi and Winston Churchill used a lot of Vision in their persuasive approaches. However, so did Hitler, Mussolini, and Napoleon.

An Ideal Influencing Profile

If it were possible to create an amalgam of all of the good characteristics of each of the styles, the person possessing this ability would be a powerful influencer—simply based on his or her ability to operate effectively in all sections of the influencing model. While it may not be practical for most of us to assume that we can achieve such an ideal, it is useful to look at what the behaviors might be. The ideal influencing style would have enough Persuasiveness to be driven to find solutions that are pragmatic and address the substantive or factual issues at hand. At the same time, it would have enough Trust in the profile to demonstrate a concern for building relationships to create long-term allies.

The person with the ideal style would carefully consider who else should be involved in the decision, and be willing to share the power and the rewards according to the needs of the situation. He or she would consult with, and ask for the opinions of, others who may be functional experts or staff members, and would not be afraid to share with other people. He or she would seriously consider, as the Control people do, the policies and procedures that would be affected by any actions or decisions that they might make, and would respect these rules and adhere to them as long as they remain functional, but would be willing to change or move outside of the rules when they felt those rules were restrictive and did not add value to the situation. They would also have enough Control behavior to be dominant when necessary, but the Control would be focused on overcoming the problem, not the other people. They could temper that strength with the ability to merge insights from different people and gain commitment to integrative solutions when the concerns of all parties can be reconciled.

This combination of Persuasion, Control, Trust, and Vision enables a moderate amount of disagreement or differing opinions on an issue to surface, and, by grappling with these issues, a more constructive and creative examination of available options can be carried out. The following guidelines are intended to help you focus on the relationship building side of influence, with an emphasis on how your style helps determine your effectiveness.

1. Be aware of your style, and get in the practice of trying to estimate or anticipate the style of others with whom you will be interacting.

2. Seek out feedback—honest, candid, specific—on your style.

3. During every interpersonal interaction, use the opportunity to try to further clarify the substantive issues and needs of the other party.

4. Try to listen to the underlying implications, and the sometimes non-verbalized needs and agendas, of others.

5. To every extent possible, maintain two-way conversations throughout. Watch for periods of time when either you or the person you're trying to influence clearly seem to be dominating the conversation. If you notice that this is the case, take action to break rhythm—whether it be your own dominance or others'.

6. Demonstrate understanding and attentiveness to the needs of the other party. Use reflective statements, paraphrasing, and empathizing to demonstrate and confirm your understanding of their position. Ask questions about their statements, to show interest and to clarify what they are really after.

7. Demonstrate your ability to be open-minded and to accept reasonable, creative alternatives to the ideas you have.

8. Work toward the creating of a problem-solving, problem-focused environment. Try to minimize emphasis on beginning positions, and spend or invest time up front in clarifying the interests of all the people involved.

9. Try to minimize personality involvement in conflicts by focusing on the issues. If you are dealing with a person you genuinely do not like, extra effort must be given to keep the focus on substantive issues. You don't need to like the people you are working with, but you may be required to continue dealing with them as colleagues.

10. As appropriate, ask for advice regarding alternatives and cre-
    ative solutions to the issues that you have posed. If suggestions
    on these issues are offered, recognize and reinforce these con-
    tributions, and build upon them wherever possible rather than
    attempting to discredit the suggestions.

11. Be willing to confront conflict and/or objections directly, but
    in a constructive fashion. Focus on the substance or impact of
    the conflict, rather than the personality that may be causing it.

As you come to understand your individual style, and how to make
use of it to your advantage, you will be increasingly able to interact
effectively with colleagues, clients, and others whom you need to influence, and to make them into allies.

NOTES

1. Jerome D. Frank, *Persuasion and Healing: A Comparative Study of Psychotherapy*
(New York: Schocken Books, 1961), 33.

2. Robert B. Cialdini, *Influence: The Psychology of Persuasion*, rev. ed. (New York:
Quill, William Morrow, 1993), 173.

3. Ibid.

PART II

Applying Influence

Having a clear idea of what influence is, and what the components of
an influential person are, we then need to focus our attention on how
influence operates within the workplace environment. Chapter 5—
Building Alliances—examines an approach to building an influence
base without appearing to be out of the organization's control. It points
out that being influential is not the same as being political, and shows
how to go about being influential without seeming to build an empire.
Chapter 6—Reciprocity and Influencing—discusses some of the pragmatic applications of influence strategy. It looks at the various ways in
which we can influence others through exchanges of value and persuasive approaches. Chapter 7—Influence and Persuasion—The Selling
Construct—looks at the needs satisfaction process, and how that can be
brought into play to enhance your ability to influence others when you
are presenting your need for compliance. Chapter 8—Influencing Despite Authority—covers specific skill sets and how influence plays a part
in supervision: outlining tasks, giving orders, disciplining, and providing
feedback. Chapter 9—Influencing Job Performance—shows how influence can be used to effect behavior change in the workplace through
helping to define roles and using coaching skills. Chapter 10—Influencing Up—highlights the approaches and pitfalls of dealing with organization superiors. Finally, Chapter 11—The Influencing Group Process—
demonstrates the way influence works in group settings, covering such
issues as facilitation, building allies, and surfacing risk issues.

CHAPTER 5

Building Alliances

As soon as we begin to think about how we can be influential within the organization, the issue of organizational politics becomes important. The political structure and activities within your organization will help define and determine what kinds of influencing behaviors you can engage in without running afoul of the political norms. In your attempts to develop allies, build alliances, and enhance your informal networks, you do not want to be perceived as being out of the organization's control. In your attempts to develop connections and interact more regularly and effectively, you do not want to be perceived as disloyal or insubordinate. Organizations have different tolerance levels for different types of influencing behavior. Therefore, it is extremely important to have a clear picture of the internal political system where you work.

Communication theorists define organizational politics in a variety of ways. Madison et al. call it the overt communication of power.[1] Porter, Allen, and Angle call it discretionary attempts at social influence, designed to promote or protect self-interest while threatening the self-interest of others.[2] What they are suggesting is that behavior regulation strategies, or attempts at influence, are political when they are used to expand personal power. Unlike the formal systems within organizations that restrict the types of activity that people can engage in, anyone can participate in organizational politics, and these informal political actions affect the structure, formal authority, direction, and parameters of the organization.[3]

Politics of some sort are inescapable, since all organizations contain subcultures that compete for resources, promote self-interest, and have the desire to accomplish the tasks and responsibilities assigned to them. This competition for resources causes people within the organization to take actions aimed at maintaining a political power base.

Power bases within the organization can be found at all levels. It is possible for a worker to possess a power base not held by or shared by a supervisor. Also, power is not always exerted downward. The effect of unions on the organization would be an example of power being exerted from below and influencing the outcomes of the broader organization above. Another scenario for organizational politics occurs when it involves attempts by one employee or a group of employees to make the organization accept their interpretation of a situation or event, regardless of whether tangible resources are involved.[4]

When political activity is generated in the organization, it is usually the result of circumstances that appear to challenge the power structure. Middle- and upper-level managers tend to be more involved in political activities than lower-level employees, because their jobs involve decisions that can upset or transform deeper elements of the power relationship. There is more political activity around issues such as reorganization, personnel assignment, and budget allocation. This happens because these issues are important to the organization and to individual employees. Also, they involve high levels of uncertainty.[5]

When an organization is highly structured, political activity is restrained because virtually all decisions are made through established procedures and policies. However, with organizations that are undergoing major changes (such as most organizations today), the deep structure of the organization is less constraining, and political activities are more common. Because of the current ambiguity of organizational power bases, attempts to exert influence can be perceived as offensive, manipulative, or empire-building. Managers who buy into the notion that we should look for opportunities to be more collaborative, and develop more informal network ties, may not act on these impulses because there is a fear that these efforts will be perceived in a negative way.

Common fears in this regard include being perceived as being uncontrollable: Will my manager fear a loss of control if he or she builds a partnership with me and encourages me to form strategic alliances in the organization? Could this push my boss's control buttons? Will the boss fear I'll go charging off on my own and do something dumb? Will the boss worry that there won't be a reasonable limit to how much I will push back as a partner? Will these concerns be so great that the notion of partnership is a sham, and in the last analysis will I be forced to deal with the boss—since this has to be done anyway? Will I be perceived as disloyal and insubordinate?

Some managers are very concerned with their version of loyalty, who might worry about whether I'll know the difference between healthy disagreement and disrespect. Will I cross the line, in my boss's mind, between arguing for what I think is right in an assertive way and not being a team player? My goal of expressing loyal disagreement might be seen as being insubordinate.

BEING POLITICAL

If I need to be highly influential with colleagues and negotiate agreements, will they see me as the proverbial "organization politician," forever cutting deals to get myself ahead? Will I be perceived as always looking out for what I can get, and not interested in doing the right things for the organization's sake? Will I be seen as changing my position with whichever way the wind blows?

Will I be perceived as an empire-builder? If I act as if I am not limited by my formal job description, will I be perceived as building an empire and trying to grab additional areas? What is the difference between taking initiative and grabbing turf? Will my attempts to get things done be threatening to colleagues' territory?

These are the questions that need to be asked and answered within the context of your particular organizational culture. It is a common misconception that an increase in power will create less vulnerability and more success in organizational politics. What actually happens is that increases in authority are associated with increased vulnerability; more authority and expanded influence increase the complexity of managing a power base.

One example of a shift in the power relationship is when a father begins working for a son, or a faculty member becomes a dean and consequently ends up managing his or her former chairperson. A survey done by Madison et al. indicated that managers made the following observations when asked to determine the nature of power in organizational politics:

1. Low-, middle-, and upper-level managers indicated that organizational politics is a frequently occurring activity.

2. Ninety percent of all managers agree that organizational politics occurs more frequently at the middle and upper levels than at lower levels.

3. Politics tends to occur most often in staff positions, rather than in line positions.

4. Persons in marketing are viewed as most susceptible to political power and influence activity. They are followed, in order, by the Board of Directors, Sales, and Manufacturing.

5. Desirable moves in the organization are perceived to occur through politics.

6. Nearly all respondents believe that politics could be harmful; all believe that politics could be helpful.

They also asked managers what characteristics were exhibited by those seen as effective in organizational politics, and discovered the following:

1. *Blaming or attacking others.* Blaming is either reaction to a situation or anticipatory in nature; reactive behavior centers on scapegoating, whereas proactive blaming contains more personal content directed at reducing competition for scarce resources.

2. *Use of information.* Competition leads competitors to withhold and/or distort information when interacting. Likewise, individuals may avoid situations that require disclosure of unfavorable information.

3. *Creation and maintenance of a favorable image.* The utilization of nonverbal behavior to communicate sensitivity to appearance, organization, adherence to norms, attention to success, and being on the inside are deemed as effective actions.

4. *Developing a base of support.* Common practice among many organizational groups is to conduct an informal private pre-meeting prior to the actual announced meeting. This process encourages participants to form coalitions prior to the scheduled meeting. Further, the informal meeting commits participants to a plan of action before agenda items are discussed publicly. This activity fosters, among those who do not participate in the pre-

meeting, a perception of solidarity within the coalition, whether real or imagined.

5. *Ingratiation.* By communicating feelings of esteem toward another party, the source of esteem satisfies another's feelings of self-worth.

6. *Development of strong allies.* Power players seek out and endeavor to maintain professional and social relationships with others who possess power.

7. *Forming power coalitions.* Associating with others in power increases one's individual power base. Power coalitions are not limited to fellow employees; coalitions extend beyond the organizational environment, and include fellow members of professional associations, country clubs, and other social groups.[6]

Some of these strategies could be considered outright aggressive or hostile. In general, the softer influence strategies—like being only persuasive, or using ingratiation—seem to be more effective in persuading other employees to change their beliefs or actions than harder strategies.[7]

The choice of influence strategies seems to depend on several factors: the particular goal—the status of their influence target—and the point in the influence effort. If a person's goal is to improve someone's performance, or to get another individual or group of individuals to help meet organizational objectives, cooperative strategies are more common. When the objective is to get personal assistance or rewards, ingratiation tends to be the most common strategy.[8]

Other research indicates that when the target person has high formal status, rational argument is the most common choice—that is, from a style perspective, we would tend to be Persuasive. When the target is of low status, more Competitive and Manipulative strategies seem to come into play.

A study of supervisors' personal preferences points out that a supervisor's choice of influence strategy depends to a large extent on how he or she feels about the subordinate. They use friendly and attractive compliance strategies with subordinates whose communication is friendly and attractive, and they use unattractive strategies with subordinates who communicate in unattractive ways. "Unattractive" in this case could be interpreted as a mismatch in styles, thus helping to validate the conclusion of Chapter 4.[9] It is reasonable to extend the same conclusion—that is, that supervisors really do engage in preferential treatment of subordinates whom they like—to the interaction between colleagues. As with everything else about organizational communication, this choice of influence strategies is reciprocal.

BUILDING YOUR INFORMAL NETWORK

Conventional approaches tend to place influence behaviors within the broader context of organizational politics. Certainly, the application of both power and influence comes into play in the political arena. However, influence as we are describing it here does not require politics in order to be effective, and all acts of influence do not—by definition—become political.

Focusing again for a moment on the changing workplace attitudes, it becomes apparent that as our view of the organization changes, we develop different priorities. We need to become less dependent and more self-promoting within the organization, and to keep a clear eye on the world outside the organization.

To be a career thriver, you need to renew your dedication and commitment to your individual strengths and talents, and to develop an inner security core. You need to realize that no one person or organization can take this away unless you let them. If you have a well-developed loyalty to your career, you go a long way to being a successful player in the organizational arena. You will contract to provide expertise and loyalty to the corporation for a specified or unspecified period of time. You can contribute the best of your talents to the success of the organization because you are the best that you can be.

After a re-engineering or downsizing, the remaining members of the staff are frequently thrust into new roles, and new patterns of communication and interaction with one another. One day the company does business as it always has within a traditional hierarchical structure, with employees knowing exactly what tasks they are responsible for and to whom they are accountable. The next day segments of middle management are let go; the hierarchical ladder is flattened, and the survivors are quickly told to discard their old jobs and their outdated ways of working, while being introduced to colleagues on their new, self-managing teams. Under these circumstances it is unreasonable to expect people to rapidly exchange one communication and work structure for another. As an organization begins to undergo a total change process, the power of the formalized networks starts to ebb—largely because of the uncertainty of management authority and influence during this unstable period.

While the formal networks remain weakened and in a dynamic state during times of organizational change, the informal networks of an organization often gain in strength and numbers, particularly as previously powerful members of the formal networks greatly diminish in force. How you perform and communicate within the loose structure of these informal networks will be largely responsible for the degree of your continued success.[10]

Since one of the most prominent ways we can gather and assert influence in an organization is through the acquisition of information and the ability to dispense that information to appropriate individuals, it is very important to know with whom to speak, and what channels to utilize. Also, the development of good working relationships with colleagues at all levels will help you achieve your goals. By learning the rules and structures of the organization, and establishing effective interpersonal relationships, you can help direct activities within bureaucratic organizations, rather than being manipulated by the bureaucratic structure. Therefore, your quest for additional influence begins with enhancing your network contacts, particularly your informal communication networks.

A network is a grouping of organizational members who engage in patterned interaction. Gary Kreps, in his book *Organizational Communication*, identifies three types of communication networks:

1. *Total system networks*. These networks map the patterns of communication throughout the entire organization.
2. *Clique networks*. These networks identify groups of individuals within the organization who communicate more exclusively with one another than with other organization members.
3. *Personal networks*. These networks include the individuals who often interact with a given organization member.

In the sphere of influence, it is most important to expand our understanding of personal networks. Kreps goes on to divide personal networks into two types.

Personal networks can be of two types: radial and interlocking. In radial personal networks, an individual interacts with other organization members who do not generally interact with one another, while in interlocking personal networks, all the members interact.

Because all members of an interlocking personal network are connected by patterned communication, they are said to have a high level of communication "integration."[11]

The interlocking aspect of personal networks is considered integrated because of the strong ties among network members. These members have a great deal of communication contact with one another, and often are similar to one another in terms of job category and the like.

THE THEORY OF WEAK TIES

This brings us back to the "weak ties" theory again. Personal networks also contain interactions among individuals who rarely have communication contact with one another, and this is indicative of weak ties.

Recall that the theory of weak ties suggests that the information strength of weak network ties is greater than the information strength of strong ties. That is, people who do not generally interact tend to have more new information that is of value to one another than do individuals who communicate with one another quite often. This presents a paradox. It is easier to communicate with those who are most like oneself than it is to establish effective relationships with those who are very different. For example, consider the many difficulties in interpersonal communication in intercultural settings. The main implication of the theory of weak ties for organization members, though, is that it is worth the effort to establish new and different communication relationships in organizations because weak ties can provide organization members with insightful perspectives on organizational life and build the necessary base of allies to increase influence.[12]

Researchers looking into the way communication networks form and interact have identified several network roles. These are the most common:

- *Isolates*. Isolates are individuals who rarely have contact with other people in the organization. This may be due to the fact that they are avoiding others within the organization or, on the other hand, are being avoided. In those instances where the same individual may belong to more than one clique, that person could be perceived as an isolate in one clique and carry a completely different role in another clique.

- *Opinion Leaders.* Opinion leaders are members of an informal network who provide a leadership role. While it is possible they have a formal authority in the organization, it is not necessary. They tend to influence the behaviors of other organization members, as well as the decisions that are made.

- *Gate Keepers.* Gate keepers are individuals who facilitate and restrict the flow of information between members of the organization. They are in a position to make judgments about who should get which information, and when. Often they play the role of channeling only important information to people in primary leadership roles.

- *Cosmopolites.* Cosmopolites have access both inside and outside of the organization. They are the people who connect the organization with other organizations and with its environment. They gather information from outside sources and bring that information back to the organization, enabling the organization to change and adapt to the changing need of the environment. Cosmopolites are also the primary external communicators. They carry the organization's message to the environment.

- *Bridges.* Bridges connect one clique to another within the organization. Their primary function is to see that essential information is shared between various departments and other substructures in the organization, so that the large organization can function efficiently and effectively. Often, organizations try to formalize bridge roles, as in a matrix management system. However, the most successful bridge interactions continue to occur on an informal basis.

- *Liaisons.* While liaisons perform roles similar to bridges, they do not themselves belong to any specific clique. They often find themselves in the role of gathering essential information from two cliques and disseminating it both ways, rather than the more typical bridge, who would have the information of one clique and carry it to another.

Figure 5.1 represents a typical organizational chart that illustrates the formal reporting lines, and by extension the formal communication patterns, within an organization. Our organization chart illustrates the prescribed formal relationships among the organization's members, based on their job responsibilities. It graphically presents the reporting rela-

Figure 5.1
Organizational Chart

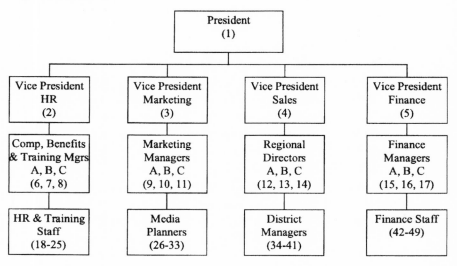

tionships, and who supervises whom, as well as those with whom a particular organization member works directly.

Under the best of conditions, communication in informal structures moves downward, upward, and horizontally. However, as most of us have experienced, many organizations over-utilize the downward communication channels, which become over-burdened with messages—orders, directives, and guidelines—that often conflict with one another. If formal communication structures and strategies are going to be effective in the organization—whether downward, upward, or horizontal—the most important factor is the development of meaningful interpersonal relationships among organizational members. These interpersonal relationships form the basis of an informal message-flow system. Informal message-flow is the communication that develops among organization members that is not necessarily prescribed by the formal structure and hierarchy of the organization. It grows out of the individual organization member's curiosity, interpersonal attraction, and social interaction.

Informal communication systems develop within an organization because of the members' need for information about the organization, and how changes in the organization will affect their lives. As we have pointed out earlier, because of the disruption in the formal organizational patterns due to reorganization, downsizing, and other initiatives, the need for information through information networks has been com-pounded.

Those individuals who lack powerful, formal, hierarchical positions within the organization, but have succeeded in gathering key informa-tion about the organization and other members of the organization, and are effective at disseminating that information on an as-needed basis, become informal leaders. These informal leaders wield a great deal of influence, but are not necessarily recognized by the formal power struc-ture of the organization as being either legitimate or influential. At its extreme, informal leadership becomes destructive. Some people who do not have formal positions of power within organizations seek power informally by gathering information of high interest to others. By de-veloping a stockpile of relevant information and bartering this infor-mation for favors rendered by other organization members, they develop the ability to influence the behavior of others within the organization, generally for their own benefit.

Perhaps as a result of this negative behavior, informal communica-tion—or "the grapevine," as it is generally called—is viewed negatively by a lot of people. Many feel that the grapevine is primarily concerned with gossip and promoting rumors that injure reputations and hurt peo-ple's feelings. However, while admittedly there is negative impact from some aspects of informal communication, in today's organization it is more often the opposite position that holds true—that is, informal com-munication systems carry more important information to individuals, and are more helpful to individuals, than the formal systems.

Attempts to restrict informal communication serve to increase organ-ization members' ambiguities and need for relevant information. There is a direct relationship between the need for information and the growth of the grapevine. Today's organizations, many with climates of high un-certainty, provide fertile ground for the growth of informal communi-cation systems, and in fact these systems provide an important function.

Also, contrary to what one might think, the quality of the information in informal communication channels is generally more accurate. Informal channels have less distortion because of the many opportunities for feed-back. This provides a system of checks and balances for information coming in. Davis and O'Connor suggest that there are fewer risks in providing accurate information in the informal systems, primarily be-cause there are fewer status discrepancies.[13] The challenge for the man-ager who will exert the necessary influence to get his or her work done in today's workplace is to first analyze the type of informal communi-

Figure 5.2
Network Chart

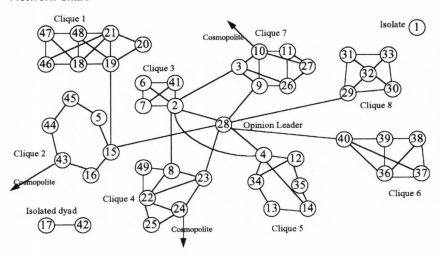

cation networks that are in operation at the organization, and then to take on those roles that will provide the greatest return for the effort.

Figure 5.2 illustrates one possible informal network scheme that relates to the formal network scheme presented in Figure 5.1.

Several cliques are presented, aligned around the appropriate members. However, opportunities for opinion leaders and bridges are also shown. It should be obvious that, if you are to become an effective influencer in the organization, you are going to have to increase your bridge behavior, as well as your cosmopolite behavior, and—if possible—try to develop as an opinion leader in the informal network structure.

INVENTORY FOR BUILDING A COMMUNICATION STRATEGY

Here are several questions which you can ask yourself to help determine how well you are doing as an informal network communicator, and the directions you need to look in to enhance your effectiveness:

- Do I have a clear idea of what I want to accomplish with a network?

- Do I know what potential allies need? And if not, how do I find out?

- Do I have resources that would be of interest to others?

- Are my internal relationships positive enough to make transactions possible and relatively easy?

- Does my interaction style fit with the preferred style of my potential allies?

- Can I change my style and still be true to myself?

- Am I contacted frequently for advice or support?

- Do I make an effort to get together with colleagues on a regular basis?

- Do I volunteer to sit on task forces or committees, to get to know higher-level managers or peers from other functional areas?

- Have I established a good working relationship with at least one key member of each function or area?

- Do I periodically attend professional conferences and make contacts with other key people in my industry and other industries?

- Do I regularly attend company social events?

When you have completed an inventory of both your prevailing operating and interaction style and the type and structure of the informal networks in your organization, you are ready to set forth in the process of building allies.

NETWORKING STYLE INVENTORY (NSI)

For a quick index of your networking style, complete the *Networking Style Inventory* in Appendix A. The NSI is designed to give you a quick index of basic characteristics associated with networking behavior and attitudes. It uses the common marketplace terms of Retailer, Wholesaler, Entrepreneur, and Street Vendor to describe various modalities of "selling yourself" in the organization. Ideally, we would want to fall in the Wholesaler-Entrepreneurial range in order to take advantage of today's organizational climate.

A recent study of 200 middle managers using the NSI showed that 85 percent of them were acting like "Street Vendors":

- Removal from other managers
- Using quick fixes
- Not following up
- Looking for reasons why problems can't be solved

If we continue to allow the stresses and ambiguities rampant in our organizational lives to drive us into deeper isolation, we will not be able to develop and exert the necessary influence for personal and organizational success.

DEVELOPING AND USING A PERSONAL SUPPORT NETWORK

As we have discussed, every manager needs a personal support network in order to be influential. In fact, one way of acquiring, maintaining, and demonstrating your interpersonal competence is to have a network of supportive relationships that can be drawn upon as needed to help you achieve your particular objectives. A well-developed support network includes a variety of types of individuals and is not limited to people who are close to you or good listeners or advice givers.

Members of your informal support network may not be aware that they are part of your system, and they may or may not be aware of others in the network. These relationships may be close and personal or distant and formal; but they must be equitable, fair, related to material and emotional support, able to provide essential information or access, and accepting of reciprocal behaviors on your part.

Building a support network begins with an inventory of people or functions that could potentially provide significant support to your efforts. Appendix B provides an inventory that walks the manager through the process of analyzing the current support network and building a more effective network. Since the larger the network, the more effort is required to maintain it, careful selections need to be made. Another factor involves risk. There is always the potential for being rejected by people who, for a variety of reasons, do not want to be part of your support network. Perhaps the key influencing strategy for building this network is the exchange of value based on the reciprocity rule.

Charles Seashore has identified seven types of support network members:

- *Role Models*—People who present behavior and help define goals one might aspire to attain. Role models show what is possible and are a source of valuable information about opportunities and obstacles associated with a given role.

- *Commom Interests*—People who share the same vision or concerns. They can be counted on to help sort out those problems that are primarily imposed by the larger system and that require collective activity to bring about changes.

- *Close Friends*—People who help provide nurturing and caring, who enjoy some of the same interests, and who keep one from becoming isolated and alienated.

- *Helpers*—People who can be depended upon to provide assistance. These people are often experts in solving particular kinds of problems and may not be the type with whom one would choose to have a close personal relationship.

- *Respect Competence*—Individuals who respect the skills one has already developed and who value the contributions that one makes in a given situation.

- *Referral Agents*—People who can provide access to resources in the organization through their knowledge of people and the organization, where needed assistance can be obtained.

- *Challengers*—People who provide motivation to explore new ways of doing things, develop new skills, and work toward the development of latent capabilities. They often are people who one may not care for as personal friends, and who can be abrasive and demanding.[14]

Often the same person plays more than one role in a support system.

Support networks provide a springboard for influence because they nurture a feeling of belonging and acceptance, enhance our confidence and competence, and provide various means for managing problems. Our individual needs for support change as our lives change. So, support networks are dynamic and change as the individual's needs change.

Unfortunately, however, we often do not derive sufficient support from such networks. Most organizations develop competitive environments; thus, most of us know relatively few people at work with whom we can discuss problems in depth. In the fast-paced and changeable environment of a large corporation, frequent changes in staffing and job assignments make relationship building even more difficult. In addition, since departments are so interdependent, they often view each other with suspicion, or feel that others are more of a source of problems than a potential help. Therefore, to have good quality networks of supportive relationships, most of us have to create them consciously, or at least work at improving some of our present relationships.

It is instructive to make a list of people considered part of your current network and associate those names with each of the seven categories above.

- What sources of support are currently absent from your network?
- Are a few people associated with several categories?
- Are there people who should be part of your support network that are currently not listed?
- What is the size of the support network?
- What do I call upon my support network to provide most often?

Building a functioning support network and establishing alliances are the foundation of a manager's influencing efforts. They provide resources to get the work done, a forum for sharing information and problem solving, and relationships that open access to others in the organization.

Networks and alliances are not provided by the organization. They must be carefully built and nurtured if one is to accomplish the work required by a complex system that cannot always be understood or controlled.

NOTES

1. Dan Madison et al., "Organizational Politics," *Human Relations* 33 (1980), 79–100.

2. Lyman W. Porter, Robert W. Allen, and Harold L. Angle, "The Politics of Upward Influence in Organizations," in *Organizational Influence Processes*, edited by R. W. Allen and L. W. Porter, eds. (Glenview, IL: Scott, Foresman, 1983), 408–422.

3. M. L. Tushman, "A Political Approach to Organizations: A Review and Rationale," in *Organizational Influence Processes*, edited by R. W. Allen and L. W. Porter (Glenview, IL: Scott, Foresman, 1983), 393–407.

4. Gail Fairhurst, L. Edna, and Robert Sarr, *Manager-Subordinate Control Pat-*

terns and Judgments about the Relationship, Communication Yearbook 10, edited by Margaret McLaughlin (Beverly Hills, CA: Sage, 1987).

5. Victor Thompson, *Modern Organizations* (New York: Knopf, 1967).

6. D. L. Madison et al., "Organizational Politics: An Exploration of Managers' Perceptions," in *Organizational Processes*, edited by R. W. Allen and L. W. Porter (Glenview, IL: Scott, Foresman, 1983), 455–474.

7. Cecilia Falbe and Gary Yukl, "Consequences of Managers Using Single Influence Tactics and Combinations of Tactics," *Academy of Management Journal* 32 (1992), 638–652.

8. Young Kim and Katherine Miller, "The Effects of Attributions and Feedback on the Generation of Supervisor Feedback Message Strategies," *Management Communication Quarterly* 4 (1990): 6–29.

9. Michael Garko, "Persuading Subordinates Who Communicate in Attractive and Unattractive Styles," *Management Communication Quarterly* 5 (1992), 289–315.

10. Marvin R. Gottlieb and Lori Conkling, *Managing the Workplace Survivors: Organizational Downsizing and the Commitment Gap* (Westport, CT: Quorum Books, 1995).

11. Gary L. Kreps, *Organizational Communication: Theory and Practice* (New York: Longman, 1986), 218.

12. Ibid.

13. W. Davis and J. R. O'Connor, "Serial Transmission of Information: A Study of the Grapevine," *Journal of Applied Communication Research* 5 (1977), 61–72.

14. Charles E. Seashore, "Developing and Using a Personal Support System," in *The Reading Book for Human Relations Training*, edited by Larry Porter (NTL Institute for Applied Behavioral Sciences, 1979).

CHAPTER 6

Reciprocity and Influencing

One of the major building blocks of human relationships is reciprocity. The rule of reciprocity states that, when something is received from another, we should try to repay it in kind. Reciprocity forms the basis of the extrinsic influencing strategies.

Our behaviors, in relation to one another, are then influenced in response to the way each behaves. When one person fulfills the expectations of another, it encourages that person to fulfil the expectations of the initiator. This affects the way we communicate with each other as well. If we perceive that a person is communicating with us on a personal basis, we are then more likely to respond in the same way. W. W. Wilmot suggests that the reciprocity factor increases in interpersonal relationships incrementally over time. The more you fulfill certain expectations of someone else, the more likely that person is to fulfill your expectations. For example, you may begin by doing a simple favor for a co-worker, such as asking if he or she would like a cup of coffee when you are making a trip to the coffee room. This behavior acknowledges an awareness of the other person, and would be likely to increase that person's awareness of you.

The rule of reciprocity suggests that, in the future, that person will be inclined to do a favor for you as well—either the same favor of getting you coffee or some similar service that would be considered at the same level of commitment. It says that if the two of you have entered into a contract, over time the opportunity might arise for you to help this individual with a more difficult task, and it is likely—when you do that—somewhere down the line, this person will be willing to reprioritize your needs and help you with a difficult task.[1]

Robert Cialdini also deals in some detail with the rule of reciprocation. In discussing the power of reciprocation, he talks about how universal its effect is:

> The impressive aspect of the rule for reciprocation and the sense of obligation that goes with it is its pervasiveness in human culture. It is so widespread that, after intensive study, sociologists such as Alvin Gouldner can report that there is no human society that does not subscribe to the rule. And within each society it seems pervasive also; it permeates exchanges of every kind. Indeed, it may well be that a developed system of indebtedness flowing from the rule for reciprocation is a unique property of human culture.[2]

Archaeologists and cultural anthropologists, such as Richard Leakey, Lionel Tiger, and Robin Fox, point to the fact that human beings have developed a network of obligation and a web of indebtedness, and that this exchange mechanism is unique to human beings, allowing for the division of labor, the exchange of diverse forms of goods, the exchange of different service, and the creation of a cluster of interdependencies that bind individuals together into highly efficient units.[3] As a behavioral construct, this becomes an important tool of influence, since the rule of reciprocation enables one person to take the first step, or to provide help, resources, or other exchangeable items with another individual with some reasonable expectation that someday he or she will be repaid.

In one experiment done by Professor Dennis Regan of Cornell University, subjects participating in the study were asked to rate, along with another person, the quality of some paintings as part of an experiment on art appreciation. The other person, in each case, was Dr. Regan's assistant, who was actually part of the experiment. During the course of the experiment, the assistant found opportunities to do small favors for the subject of the experiment. For example, he would leave the room for a couple of minutes and return with two bottles of Coca-Cola—one for the subject and one for himself—saying, "I asked if it was all right to get myself a Coke, and they said it was OK, so I brought one for you, too." In other cases, the assistant did not provide the other subject with a favor. He simply returned after the break and went back to work.

When all the paintings had been rated, the assistant then asked the subject if he would be willing to buy some raffle tickets that he was selling, so that he could win a $50 prize. The major finding of this study shows that the number of tickets varied depending on whether or not the assistant had done a favor for the subject. Apparently, feeling that they owed him something, the subjects for whom he had done a favor bought twice as many tickets as the subjects who had not been given the prior favor.

The other part of the finding was that it apparently didn't matter whether or not they responded favorably to the assistant on a personal level. The subjects were given a rating scale indicating how much they liked the assistant. Those responses were compared to the number of tickets they had purchased. For those who owed the assistant a favor, it apparently made no difference whether they liked him or not. They felt a sense of obligation to repay him, and they did.[4] Other examples show how the reciprocity rule works for groups soliciting in airports and elsewhere, such as the Krishnas, and how the principal also functions in the political arena. As this book is being prepared, a major investigation has been undertaken to determine whether or not the gift from the Chinese government to the Democratic Party may have influenced the policy on preferred nation status.

In their book *Influence without Authority*, Allen Cohen and David Bradford provide a management example of the same reciprocity rule. Discussing how general managers tend to help each other out through reciprocal arrangements, Cohen and Bradford point out that various divisions of a large company often absorb each others' excess costs or profits each quarter, because they are being judged by headquarters on how well they meet quarterly budgeted targets—but often the results are dependent on economic events outside their control.

> By using cross-charges to smooth results, they can work together and more readily meet their individual goals. The overall impact for profits is nil, but this kind of horsetrading allows them to save for a rainy day or borrow when in need. A general manager who refuses to cooperate in this way soon finds himself frozen out of the other forms of cooperation among the group.[5]

Cohen and Bradford base a large portion of their approach to influencing on the exchange method. Exchange provides some very useful constructs, and these are incorporated in the influencing model as extrinsic influencers. In some cases the exchange approach drifts across the shadowy line between influence and negotiation. There are three forms of exchange:

- *Compliance for mutual benefit*. In this case, a person complies with your request because it is also in his own best interest, and the benefits of going along are at least as great as the cost of complying.
- *Compensation for costs*. In this instance, he will be expected to cover the costs incurred if the other party complies with your request. For example, if a request you are making requires a colleague to keep people in his or her department working overtime, as an exchange you may be required to pick up the resulting additional costs from your budget.
- *Equivalent payment*. In this form of exchange, you will be offering something to someone that is at least as valuable as what you request. Your payment must be perceived by the recipient as equivalent in value to that which you request. This is a very common form of exchange in negotiation, and is generally referred to as a "trade-off." Trading off is the process of weighing, sorting, evaluating, and deciding which of all possible options will work most effectively for you and the other person.[6]

All three forms of exchange also suggest that there would be negative consequences to a potential ally for not cooperating. The negative consequences associated with refusing an exchange provide much of the force behind sanction strategies. The suggestion is to emphasize the positive, since peers and superiors may have the same, or more, resources available for retaliation. Also, a negative approach can create its own form of reciprocity, where—rather than acquiring an ally—one ends up making an enemy, or at the very least setting up a situation that calls for a pay-back.

Cohen and Bradford provide a list of questions to ask yourself before you enter into an exchange:

- Am I clear on what I really want?
- Do I know what the ally needs, and if not, how do I find out?
- What resources do I have, and would any of them equate to the interests of the ally?

- Is our relationship positive enough to make transactions possible, and relatively easy?
- If not, how do I create sufficient trust to allow exchanges to take place?
- Does my interaction style fit with the preferred style of the potential ally? How much can I change my style and still be true to myself?[7]

Another thing to keep in mind is that the reciprocal interdependence that exists in all organizations will constantly present situations in which you will have to interact with many of the same individuals several times in different circumstances. This is especially true in the tumult that has become the modern organization. It is not uncommon to leave on Friday with one understanding of who the most important players are in your sphere, only to find that on Monday of the following week, many of those people have changed. Gone are the days when we could, with some assurance, keep our enemies at arm's length. More often than not, today's ally is gone tomorrow, and yesterday's enemy is our new boss. Reciprocal interdependency assumes that work communication flow should be multi-directional. The most effective people will be able to communicate upward, downward, and laterally, and—most of all—communication will be very interactive.

Reciprocity functions in the organization not just as a benign construct for developing relationships, or as repercussive, punitive actions; it is also inherent in the conflicts that inevitably arise in organizational life. The reciprocity rule suggests that those who demonstrate ethical conflict behaviors in the organization can encourage others to react ethically as well. Gary Kreps lists five behaviors that he considers ethical:

1. Arguing the specific issue at hand, rather than relying on hidden agendas or continually avoiding communicating about conflict issues.

2. Refuting a position without resorting to violence, character attacks, slander, or other overly-aggressive tactics.

3. Constructing a "reasonable" argument against your opponent's position and for your own position, rather than basing your position on rumors, unsubstantiated claims, and over-emotionalism.

4. Avoiding a win-at-all-costs mentality by keeping an open mind toward the ideas of others.

5. Keeping an open mind to new ideas and opportunities for compromise.[8]

Although it can sometimes be a source of conflict, the reciprocity rule allows for unequal exchanges of value. A small initial favor can produce a sense of obligation that will cause you to agree to a much larger payback than the original favor would have warranted.

Pointing once again to the Regan experiment, when the experiment was done in the late 1960s the price of a Coke was a dime. The average subject of that experiment, having been given a ten-cent drink, bought two of Joe's raffle tickets, and some bought as many as seven. Based on the number of raffle tickets purchased by the average subject, Joe realized a 500 percent return on his investment.[9] This willingness to reciprocate in an unequal fashion continues to operate even when the costs are higher, and over protracted periods of time. Back in the days when I thought formatting a disk was sharpening a pencil, I was in dire need of assistance in learning about purchasing and setting up my first computer. As it happened, I had a friend who was a computer whiz, and he offered to accompany me to the computer store and help me purchase my first machine. He also helped set it up, and provided me with some basic software to work with.

While I was extremely grateful for the help, and was sensitive to the fact that he put a few hours of time into this project, I was not prepared for what occurred approximately six months later when he came to me asking to borrow two thousand dollars. I can still remember the level of obligation I felt to provide him with these funds, even though at the time I was hard-pressed to part with that amount of money. Looking back, I can see that even at the time I felt that the prospects of being repaid were not very good. However, he got the money—and I'm still waiting. While I may think of this former friend as a moocher or a welsher for not paying me back, on some level I'm reasonably certain he has little or no guilt over the transaction, because in his mind it was reciprocal.

Another aspect of the reciprocity rule, one might call mutual concession. In addition to feeling an obligation to repay favors we have received, we also feel obligated to make a concession to someone who has made a concession to us. The whole concept of "splitting the difference" that seems to rule so many financial transactions grows out of this principle. If I have something to sell at a particular price, and you want to buy it—but at a lower price—you may begin by making me a lower offer. If my price is negotiable, I will counter-offer with something lower than the original price but not the price that you offered. The result generally is that you will respond to that concession by raising your price closer to my now lower price. The deal is then consummated by splitting the difference between us.

We respond the way we do to concessions because of the benefits that accrue to the society. This mutual concession is at the heart of all compromise, and is extremely important for a civilized society.

The reciprocation rule brings about mutual concession in two ways:

- It pressures the recipient of an already-made concession to respond in kind.
- The obligation to reciprocate a concession encourages the creation of socially desirable arrangements by ensuring that anyone who wants to make the first concession will not be exploited.

Cialdini makes a very specific point about how the reciprocation rule can be an effective and powerful tool.

Because the rule for reciprocation governs the compromise process, it is possible to use an initial concession as part of a highly effective compliance technique. The technique is a simple one that we can call the rejection-then-retreat technique. Suppose you want me to agree to a certain request. One way to increase your chances would be first to make a larger request of me, one that I will most likely turn down. Then, after I have refused, you would make the smaller request that you were really interested in all along.[10]

Another interesting thing about the concession process is that the second request that you make does not have to be much smaller by comparison; it only has to be smaller than the initial one.

At the risk of being morbid, a superb example of this reciprocal sequence occurs when the bereaved select a coffin in a funeral parlor. The grieving family is generally shown the most expensive and luxurious models first, so that by the time they get to the "pine box" section they feel obligated to spend much more than perhaps they had originally intended. Additional research seems to point to the fact that the recipients of such a strategy, far from feeling manipulated or resentful, feel greater responsibility for and satisfaction with the arrangement than if the strategy had not been employed. It is reasonable, then, that people who are satisfied with their first encounter of this type are more likely to agree to further such arrangements.

CURRENCIES OF EXCHANGE

Beginning with the premise that almost everyone is responsive to the reciprocation rule, one action that we can take in order to enhance our influence is to take an inventory of what it is we have to offer to potential allies in the organization. Figure 6.1 presents a model for reciprocity.

We borrow the term "currencies" from Cohen and Bradford, who define the term as follows:

> *Currencies* represent what is important to people, the general dimensions they value. We can say, for example, that a manager who will do anything to be liked by his subordinates trades in the currency of *affection*, while the boss who wants deference and admiration from her subordinates, trades in the currency of *respect*.[11]

In order to be useful as applications, the currencies that are available to you in the organization need to be made more concrete. In order to do this, we can revisit the work of Schenck-Hamlin et al. described in Chapter 3. Schenck-Hamlin et al. identified fourteen compliance-gaining strategies:

1. Ingratiation
2. Promise
3. Debt
4. Esteem
5. Allurement
6. Aversive Stimulation
7. Threat
8. Guilt
9. Warning
10. Altruism[12]

Figure 6.1
The Gottlieb Reciprocity Model

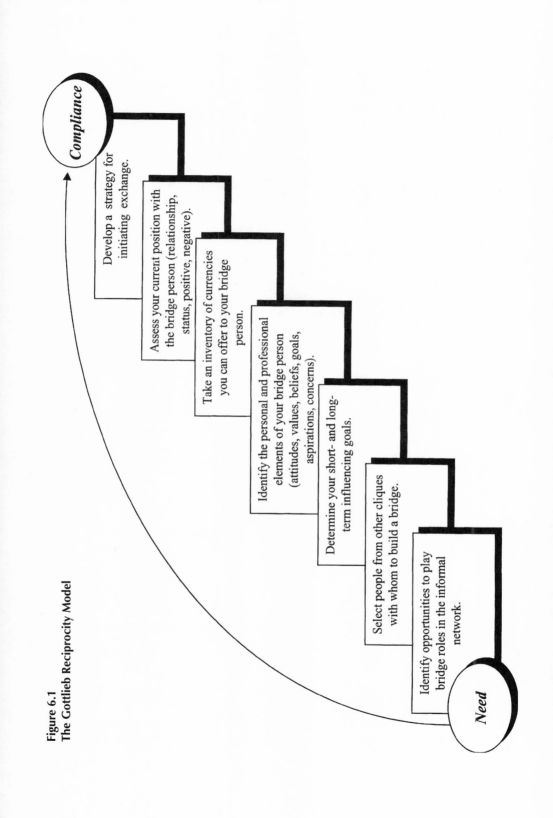

Compliance

Develop a strategy for initiating exchange.

Assess your current position with the bridge person (relationship, status, positive, negative).

Take an inventory of currencies you can offer to your bridge person.

Identify the personal and professional elements of your bridge person (attitudes, values, beliefs, goals, aspirations, concerns).

Determine your short- and long-term influencing goals.

Select people from other cliques with whom to build a bridge.

Identify opportunities to play bridge roles in the informal network.

Need

11. Direct Request

12. Explanation

13. Hinting

14. Deceit

Of the fourteen, those classified as reward appeals and altruism strategies fit most closely into the construct of reciprocity (see Table 6.1).

Table 6.1
Using Currencies Strategically

Compliance Strategy	Reasons for Compliance
Altruism—Altruism is an appeal to someone's tendency or need to be unselfish, generous, heroic, or helpful.	• Opportunity to be involved with an issue or action that is tied to the future of the organization. • An opportunity to perform beyond the commonplace. • Adhering to and satisfying the tenets of a belief system.
Promise/Debt—Promise or Debt is a presentation of what you can offer in return for compliance.	• Gaining goods or services. • Receiving a compromise on other pending issues. • Achieving settlement of debts owed.
Ingratiation/Esteem—Ingratiation and Esteem strategies provide verbal or non-verbal positive reinforcement; flattery, support, affection, or future favors.	• Potential access to other people of importance. • Feeling competent. • A sense of belonging. • Gaining visibility. • An increase in moral/ethical standing.
Allurement—Allurement presents a circumstance within which rewards are derived from others besides the influencer.	• Opportunity to provide important satisfactions to others. • Increase the level of respect and admiration. • Great potential for future rewards.

Altruism Strategies

Currencies associated with altruism create influence because they are designed to engage your potential ally in behavior that benefits you.

However, by engaging in this behavior, the ally feels better about him- or herself in a number of ways. Common approaches involve statements like: "It would help me if you would do this," and "Could you possibly do this favor for me?" or "I have a really big problem here that I believe you can help me with," or "I know if you were sitting where I am, you would be asking for help in the same way." If the potential ally does not respond to your request, the implication is that some difficulty or harm may come to you and later on, should the need arise, you might not be available to reciprocate.

Case 1

Tom Allen is a sales manager for TransPlastics, Inc. TransPlastics is a large vinyl film conversion and distribution company with offices, manufacturing facilities, and warehouses throughout the United States. Tom is in charge of the Southern Region, which covers territory that incorporates everything south of Atlanta and as far west as Houston.

Although the region has been performing well, in terms of sales, Tom feels that, because of the large geographic spread, many good sales opportunities are being lost due to insufficient personnel. Unfortunately, at this time the company is undergoing some consolidation, particularly in the Western Region, where offices and facilities are being closed. Due to the fact that layoffs are occurring, there are severe constraints on hiring throughout the organization.

Marsha Samuels, Vice President of Sales and Tom's boss, also feels the need to add some top sales people to the Southern Region. She is aware that good people have been hard to find—particularly those who are willing to travel at the level necessary to cover such a broad geographic base. She is reluctant to go against the current climate for hiring, and would have to mount a very compelling argument in order to add additional staff at this time.

On his own volition, Tom has been talking to an outstanding sales prospect, and he feels that this person won't be on the market long. He has been somewhat frustrated in his attempts to set up a meeting with Marsha, because she has been doing a great deal of traveling on her own, having to manage the consolidation problem in the West. While Tom is aware of the constraints on hiring, he just feels that this sales person would be a major addition to his staff in the Southern Region. Finally he is able to lock down a meeting with Marsha over breakfast. After some general discussion about the state of the organization, Tom makes his pitch for Marsha's compliance.

Tom: Marsha, you know I didn't set up this meeting just because I thought it would be a good idea for us to have breakfast together ... although it's a shame that there isn't more time to do just that.

Marsha: Well, I could guess that you had something important on your mind; you certainly have been persistent about getting this meeting. I'd like to apologize for having made it so difficult, but with everything going on in the West ...

Tom: I know. And I might not have been quite so persistent if the issue that I'd like to cover were not so time-sensitive.

Marsha: So, what gives?

Tom: I want to hire a top sales guy for my region.

Marsha: Tom, you know ...

Tom: Yes, I understand the issues surrounding our current hiring situation, but bear with me for a minute. When I came to work for TransPlastics, about two and a half years ago, you and I had a very serious and—I believe—defining discussion about your expectations for me and for the Southern Region.

Marsha: Yes, I remember. And you certainly have measured up.

Tom: I appreciate that. And I know we are meeting our current sales targets. But, as it stands, that's not good enough for me, and it shouldn't be good enough for you or for the company as a whole.

Marsha, we're leaving money on the table. This is just not right. With all of our current sales efforts concentrated in Miami and Tampa, we're leaving major markets like Jacksonville, Pensacola, and Houston wide open to the competition.

Marsha: Yes. I saw a report from Marketing that showed MegaFilm making inroads into Houston, particularly now that the petroleum-related industries are coming back.

Tom: That's right, and I believe there are a lot of opportunities in other areas as well. And I'm not just talking about the films business. In Jacksonville, there are major trucking operations that use a variety of packaging materials, many of which are plastic-based or could be, with the right kind of sales approach.

Marsha: So, what are you suggesting?

Tom: Marsha, I believe, with the right people in place, and a good deployment strategy, two years—possibly even eighteen months—

down the line, we can see a thirty percent increase in gross margin sales in the Southern Region.

Marsha: Wow! That's very impressive, Tom. You'd better be careful I don't hold you to that.

Tom: With my current staff, that vision will remain a fantasy. We're already spread as thin as we can possibly be, just covering the major accounts, and particularly those that need a lot of hand-holding. You know who I'm talking about.

Marsha: Absolutely. And I agree with your policy of providing very close-fitting customer service.

Tom: Marsha, I need to get another guy in the field.

Marsha: And you found someone.

Tom: And I found someone. [Tom reaches into his briefcase and pulls out a resume, which he passes across the table to Marsha.] Bob Michaels is currently working with the Northeastern Films Group for MegaPlastics. He was relocated from Houston a year and a half ago to, supposedly, head up a new product category. I believe it involves some new type of print-on material that MegaPlastics is having some difficulty perfecting. In the meantime, Bob has relocated his family to temporary quarters in Boston, but he has not as yet been successful at selling his house in Houston. His family would like very much to move back to Houston, and Bob is seriously considering it if he gets a substantial offer from us.

Marsha: Have you made him an offer?

Tom: Marsha, I wouldn't make anybody an offer without first talking to you. I did provide what I thought were some reasonable ballpark figures, and I told him that I would get back to him to hammer out something more specific after I had a chance to talk it over with you.

Marsha: Your Mr. Michaels looks very impressive on paper.

Tom: Marsha, I've made three new hires in the two and a half years that I've been here. One was a replacement, and two were brand new. You backed me on every one of those hires, and—as you know—they are all winners. I know this isn't easy; that you're going to catch a lot of flack from Mark—but you've been around long enough to know that a move like this, at the right time, that nets the kind of gains we're looking at, will just enhance your reputation as a top decision-maker.

Marsha: OK, Tom, you've got my interest. You can stop kissing up.

Tom: It never hurt.

Marsha: (laughing) Look. If I go to bat for you on this one, the goods better be there at the end.

Tom: I know . . .

Marsha: Now, Tom . . . I'm not kidding. You write this up. You give me a reasonable amount of time, during which we set and meet some specific performance targets. I'm not talking about eighteen months to two years. If I take this upstairs, I've got to be able to show that we can add business here in the fourth quarter. You put together a package and an incentive plan for your Bob Michaels that makes it clear that, if he doesn't fly, he hits the street.

Tom: Marsha, I feel so strongly about this I'm willing to stake a portion of my own bonus on the success of this move.

Marsha: Oh, don't worry about that, Tom . . . That's a given. Also, I may need you to come to Chicago to help make this pitch.

Tom: You've got it. I'll get you something on paper by the end of the week. And, Marsha, I want you to know that your support here means a lot to me. And I know if you were sitting where I am, you'd probably be making the same requests. If there's anything that I can do . . .

Marsha: I'm sure there will be, Tom. I'll let you know.

While most situations involving influence are not purely altruistic, Tom does a good job of drawing Marsha in on two levels: what is good for the company and what is potentially good for her personally. He has come to the table prepared, having already identified his candidate. He clinches Marsha's compliance through his willingness to assume personal risk.

Promise and Debt Strategies

Promise and Debt are direct approaches to the exchange of goods or services. It could actually involve the exchange of money, the sharing of or lending of personnel, the offer of additional space, providing help with current or future projects that the ally may be involved with, offering overt backing and assistance with the implementation of the ally's projects, access to technical or organizational knowledge, and so forth. Debt strategy tends to be effective when the potential ally has already been provided with some sort of tangible favor in the past, so that what you are asking for is the reciprocity already due to you: Phrases like: "If you will recall, last year when . . ."

Case 2

Harry Stanton is a Principal at McKinley and Bone, Management Consultants, Inc. He is also the project leader for an on-going re-engineering project at a major bank. The project has been under way for six months, and everyone has been extremely busy. His team has been very dedicated and hard working, but Harry knows that several staff members are eager to get some time off. In the next three weeks, however, four very important reports are due. In addition, Harry will have to go to London for a couple of days in the next three weeks on a special assignment. He needs a full commitment from his staff during this time period.

Jean Bonner is the project leader, very capable and hard working. She was recently promoted from Associate to Manager, and has so far lived up to her promise. Harry sets a meeting with Jean to discuss the workload and scheduling. He feels very strongly that things will go well as long as Jean is there to take up the slack, and he is reluctant to delegate that kind of responsibility to anybody else on the team.

On the other hand, Jean feels that she has been working exceptionally hard, and indeed she has been putting in 16-hour days and giving up a lot of weekends. She managed to complete four major projects and received a great deal of praise, for which she was grateful, but the current month is as busy as all the others. In the hopes of getting some rest and recreation, Jean has made some tentative vacation plans. On two other occasions when Jean has made plans for a vacation, she has had to change them at Harry's request because of work priorities. However, she feels particularly motivated for this vacation, since it's a chance to spend some time with a friend in Europe whom she has not seen since college. Jean arrives at the meeting with Harry, fully prepared to request time for a two-week vacation.

Harry: Hi, Jeannie. I hope this was a good time for you. I know you have been running around like crazy the last few weeks.

Jean: It's been really crazy. I don't know why we have to produce so many updates.

Harry: Well, several people have their own particular interest in this project, and they all want different information.

Jean: Tell me about it. Anyway, I'm pretty much wrapped up on the last batch and ready for some R and R.

Harry: We've got one more.

Jean: No way.

Harry: Actually, it's four reports, and they need to be completed by September 1. So, that gives us three weeks.

Jean: Three weeks?

Harry: Problem is, I'm going to London next week for the regional meeting. Most of this is going to fall on you.

Jean: Harry, you can't do this to me. Look, last month I completed three separate projects—all last-minute stuff. I have canceled vacation plans three times this year already. I have an invite to stay with a friend for two weeks in the south of France and I'm out of here.

Harry: Jeannie, I depend on you. We can't let these reports slide this close to implementation.

Jean: Listen, I know how important this deal is to all of us, and I want to help. But we need another plan. What I can do is delegate some of this to Greg.

Harry: Greg's not up to speed on the project.

Jean: I know, but he should be. We haven't had the time to go over everything with him. I'll talk to Greg. He and I can put in some extra time in the evening over the next few days—with you as well, if possible. In the meantime, give me the specs for these reports so that I can outline the contents and prepare the format. Greg can collect the necessary data and plug the numbers into the reports. You'll be back the following week to dot the i's and cross the t's.

Harry: Do you think he can do it?

Jean: I don't see why not. Besides, this is a good chance to get him up to speed on these reports. That has got to provide dividends for us down the line.

Harry: Well . . .

Jean: Harry, we go back a ways, you and me, and you know I wouldn't turn you down if it wasn't important. I need this break.

Harry: I hear you. And you certainly deserve it. Set up a meeting with you, Greg, and me for 4:30 today, and we'll take it from there.

Jean prevails because she reminds Harry that he is already indebted to her for past efforts. She also offers some concrete exchanges, "What I can do is . . ." and takes responsibility for the success of her plan. She is direct and assertive in her approach, and sells the added benefit of "bringing Greg up to speed."

Ingratiation and Esteem Strategies

Ingratiation in this sense ranges from offering up goods, sentiments, or services prior to making the request of the potential ally, to the more common and blatant forms which are generally referred to as "apple-polishing" or "brown-nosing." Actions in this category include doing favors for the ally, providing gifts, spending time listening supportively, or offering to do favors. Using the Krishnas' approach of giving flowers to passers-by in the airport is an example provided by Cialdini of an ingratiation strategy, the idea being that, once having accepted the small gift, the person then feels obligated to provide a donation because of the reciprocity rule.

Another approach appeals to the ally's self-worth. The suggestion is that compliance with your appeal could potentially increase the ally's power, success, status, and general standing within the organization. The approach works effectively when the ally sees the opportunity to be a winner. Phrases like: "Just imagine how this is going to look down the line," or "I think you're going to feel really good about this when we achieve the objective" appeal to the ally's desire for potential future rewards.

Case 3

George Steiner is V.P. Communications at National Widgetstar, Inc. One of his major duties is to produce the annual report. In order to do this, George needs to form a committee with representatives from each of the corporate divisions. This requires finesse because serving on the committee can be time consuming and there is no additional compensation.

George targets Mellany Ramos as a potential member and takes her out to lunch. Mellany is V. P. Human Resources and can provide valuable information and support for this year's theme, "People, Products, and Professionalism." However, she is currently preoccupied with a new compensation plan.

George: Mellany, I have certainly noticed a change for the better in morale around here since the new training programs were launched.

Mellany: Thanks, George, we're very excited about how it's going. I just hope you guys continue to support the program if the stock slips.

George: I think the days of saving money by canceling training are over. We've shot ourselves in the foot enough times now to learn that lesson . . . especially when we have the kind of quality programs your people are putting on.

Mellany: Are you buttering me up for something?

George: Heartfelt buttering, but I do need a favor.

Mellany: No.

George: What?

Mellany: No. I don't want to be on the Annual Report Committee.

George: Good guess. But, hear me out. You know this year's theme, right?

Mellany: Yes, but . . .

George: People, Products, and Professionalism. People! You are our people person. I have already talked to the agency about doing a spread on the new training programs . . . and maybe one on you.

Mellany: George, I'm not giving up nights and weekends for the Annual Report when I have a new comp plan to finish and implement by first quarter next year.

George: Mellany, I need you for three meetings—OK, maybe four— and you can delegate most of the other stuff that we're going to need whether you are on the committee or not. You might as well get the credit.

Mellany: What kind of a spread on me?

George: At least a full page—breaking the glass ceiling kind of stuff. Innovation, vision, the whole nine yards.

Mellany: Three meetings?

George: Four . . . and maybe a few informal get-togethers.

Mellany: George!

George: You're my star, I knew you wouldn't let me down.

Depending on your relationship with the person from whom you are seeking compliance, you may not even need to be subtle. Most people in organizational life will quickly perceive and evaluate the worthiness of the ingratiation or esteem exchange.

Allurement

Allurement is used here in the sense intended by Schenck-Hamlin et al. to mean the presentation of circumstances within which the potential reward would arise from persons or conditions other than you. In other words, by complying with your request the ally could then find him- or herself in a circumstance which becomes satisfying or appealing to others in the organization, and the resultant feelings of satisfaction would, supposedly, yield significant rewards for the ally somewhere down the line. This can be represented by an approach such as: "When we achieve this goal, you are going to get a lot of respect for the part that you played."

Case 4

Sally James is the procurement manager for the Western Region of a financial services company. She has just been told by her finance director that computer paper costs are too high. The contract with the current supplier is up for negotiation in the next three months. She has set up a meeting with Hal Richter, the sales executive responsible for the account. Sally likes working with this supplier because their deliveries are on time and they provide a quality product. She needs to get the costs lowered for the next three months, even though the contract isn't up for renewal yet.

Sally: Hal, how are you?

Hal: Fine, Sally. I hope all is well with you. I was concerned when you said you needed a meeting right away.

Sally: I'm sorry about being mysterious, Hal, but I didn't want to get into detail on the phone. We have a situation that I'm hoping you can help me with.

Hal: I'll certainly do what I can.

Sally: I just got the word that our costs for paper are running too high. One of the items targeted is computer paper, and that's where you come in.

Hal: Sally, you've got to be kidding. We squeezed all the juice out of this deal already.

Sally: What would it take to find another ten percent for the next three monthly deliveries?

Hal: Good grief, Sally! Ten percent now! What's going to happen when we sit down to talk in three months?

Sally: Hal, let's look at what we have here. We're talking about a high volume of business, right?

Hal: Yes, but it's expensive to service your business.

Sally: Why more than anyone else?

Hal: First of all, there's a receivables issue. You guys are always thirty to forty-five days out.

Sally: I wasn't aware of that.

Hal: Secondly, on several occasions this year, your people have called for an emergency delivery before the end of the month. We have always accommodated them, but at a special cost to us. We have been writing it off as good customer service, but it's not helping our thin margin on this. How am I supposed to go back to my boss and tell him we have to cough up another ten percent?

Sally: OK, Hal. What I'm hearing is that we are building additional costs for you by being slow payers and requesting special deliveries. Am I right?

Hal: Yes.

Sally: Would you say that these factors are adding ten percent to your costs?

Hal: Probably.

Sally: OK, Hal, here's something for you to take back that I believe will fly. Also, I think it's going to look good for you down the line. First, I will personally ride herd on the receivables and guarantee that you will be paid within thirty days. Second, starting with the next delivery, ship us an additional ten cases above our usual order. This should remove the need for emergency orders and for the next two months your revenue will be higher even with a ten percent cut in cost. The last month may be a short month, but we will be in negotiation for a new contract and I will push to have all our paper consolidated with your firm. Hal, it will go a long way with me to help me out with this now.

Hal: I'm going to hold you to that.

Sally: Thanks, Hal.

Sally understands that Hal is not the decision-maker on this issue. In order to get his compliance to champion her request, she has to offer something that is substantive and will carry the potential for making Hal look like a hero to his superiors. Speeding up receivables, immediately increasing volume, and having the potential for additional business in the near future provide the necessary potential to gain Hal's compliance.

VALUING RECIPROCITY

As Cialdini points out, the trade-offs or exchanges that people make are not necessarily of equal value. However, a very important point to keep in mind is that value is in the eye of the beholder. Understanding the value of each of your strategic options, as they may be viewed by the potential ally, is a key factor in your influencing success strategy.

You may not value one particular currency very highly, whereas the other person may see it as crucial. On the other hand, the opposite might be the case. For example, you might see providing tacit support for your potential ally's project as a minor currency for exchange, because your tendency would be to support the other's position anyway. However, if the ally is not aware of your supportive position, in the course of the exchange of value, that support, offered up in the proper manner at the correct time, can be a very powerful motivator toward compliance. So, reciprocity forms the foundation for our extrinsic influencing behaviors. Once again, our knowledge of the other person's needs, expectations, goals, and objectives provides the springboard toward developing a climate for compliance.

NOTES

1. W. W. Wilmot, *Dyadic Communication*, 2d ed. (Reading, MA: Addison-Wesley, 1980).

2. Robert B. Cialdini, *Influence: The Psychology of Persuasion*, rev. ed. (New York: Quill, William Morrow, 1993), 18.

3. Lionel Tiger and Robin Fox, *The Imperial Animal* (New York: Holt, Rinehart and Winston, 1971).

4. Cialdini, *Influence*, 20–21. A full report of the findings of the study can be found in Dennis T. Regan, "Effects of a Favor and Liking on Compliance," *Journal of Experimental Social Psychology* 7 (1971), 627–639.

5. Allen R. Cohen and David L. Bradford, *Influence without Authority* (New York: Wiley, 1990), 29.

6. For a more extensive discussion of trade-offs and the exchange of value during the negotiating process, see Marvin Gottlieb and William J. Healy, *Making Deals: The Business of Negotiating* (New York: New York Institute of Finance, 1990).

7. Cohen and Bradford, *Influence without Authority*, 34.

8. Gary L. Kreps, *Organizational Communication: Theory and Practice* (New York: Longman, 1986), 189.

9. Cialdini, *Influence*, 34.

10. Ibid., 38.

11. Cohen and Bradford, *Influence without Authority*, 75.

12. William Schenck-Hamlin, Richard L. Wiseman, and G. N. Georgacarakos, "A Typology and Formal Model of Compliance-Gaining Strategies," International Communication Association Convention, Acapulco, Mexico, May 1980.

CHAPTER 7

Influence and Persuasion—The Selling Construct

Of all the types of influence that we are subjected to, and the circumstances that bring it about, by far the most common influence activity occurs around the selling process. Much of what we have discussed in regard to intrinsic influencing capability also comes to bear on sales influence. However, our primary focus in this chapter is on what we call the "strategic influencers." By "strategic" we mean the ordering of events in the presentation of a message designed to influence. It really doesn't matter whether the setting for the influence is the used car lot, the broker's office, or the clergyman's study. If the intent is to alter someone's attitudes, values, beliefs, or actions, somebody is selling.

At its simplest level, selling is not a complicated process. Consider the following dialogue:

A person enters a store.

Salesperson: Can I help you?

Customer: Yes. I need a widget.

Salesperson: I have a widget.

Customer: I'll take it.

Salesperson: Here it is. That will be ten dollars.

Customer: Here is ten dollars.

Salesperson: Thank you.

This simple transaction illustrates all of the elements at the core of a selling situation. A customer has a need for something, seeks out a source for that need, and finds a likely means for satisfying that need. Another person is able to provide what the customer wants, delivers it in a satisfactory fashion, and the customer leaves with the need satisfied, while having compensated the salesperson for providing it. As simple as this transaction appears, it is often cloaked in some very complicated apparel. Motives, attitudes, and barriers of various kinds can interfere with the direct and simple need-satisfaction transaction. When we are using strategic influence in order to sell a potential ally on the idea of supporting us, we need to keep in mind that—no matter how complex the situation appears on the surface—underneath there is this simple transaction.

There is nothing particularly new about the selling construct. Aristotle discussed it, from a theoretical point of view, over two thousand years ago. In 1938, E. C. Tolman put this selling transaction in theoretical form and expressed it as a mathematical equation: $p = f(n, \exp. v)$; that is, the particular performance or choice an individual makes ("p") depends on the amount of effort he or she is willing to expend ("f") in addressing (1) the motivation at the time ("n": need); (2) the extent or probability that an action or attempted action will lead to a goal or value ("exp.": expectancy); and (3) the importance or satisfaction that goal or value has for the person ("v": value).[1] Effective influencing behavior elicits behavioral change on the part of someone else. In order for that to happen, it must be arousing and relevant to the individual's needs.

MASLOW'S HIERARCHY OF NEEDS

Before we can turn our attention to discovering the specific needs of the person we are trying to influence, we should have a good understanding of needs in general and how they function in this context. Most management people today have encountered the work of Abraham Maslow. Maslow arranged a list of needs into a hierarchy. Needs, as Maslow sees them, are bound in an integrated system based on the relative importance of the satisfaction of the needs. Higher-order needs do not develop until lower-order needs are minimally satisfied. Maslow's hierarchy, beginning with the most basic need, progresses toward more complex and sophisticated needs. These include the following:

- Physiological needs: food, water, sleep, air—basic survival needs
- Safety needs: protection from harm or injury
- Love and belonging needs: warmth, status, acceptance, approval
- Esteem needs: adequacy, self-esteem, competence
- Self-actualization needs: self-fulfillment; ideal and real self in close harmony; broader understanding and appreciation[2]

Maslow was not examining the modern organization. His assumption was that as we move up the hierarchy, we leave the previous needs behind as being satisfied. However, today's top executives know that rather than being a hierarchy, needs are cumulative. That is, one may be operating on a level of competence and esteem, but remains ever mindful that the basic survival needs are still palpable. Certainly, basic physiological needs come into play if you are entering into an exchange of value, such as the sign I have often thought of putting around my neck and sitting outside in front of my building that says, "Will write for food."

When sanction strategies are employed, the reverse might be true in the sense that a person's basic physiological and safety needs may potentially be diminished or removed if he or she does do not comply with the request at hand.

MURRAY'S LIST OF MANIFEST NEEDS

The hierarchical arrangement of needs is not the only way to see them. H. A. Murray attempts to distinguish one type of need from another, and arranges his list in alphabetical order:

Abasement. To surrender. To comply and accept punishment. To apologize, confess, atone. Self-depreciation. Masochism.

Achievement. To overcome obstacles. To exercise power. To strive to do something difficult as well and as quickly as possible.

Acquisition. To gain possessions and property. To grasp, snatch, or steal things. To bargain or gamble. To work for money or goods.

Affiliation. To form friendships and associations. To greet, join, and live with others. To cooperate and converse sociably with others. To love. To join groups.

Aggression. To assault or injure. To belittle, harm, blame, accuse, or maliciously ridicule a person. To punish severely. Sadism.

Autonomy. To resist influence or coercion. To defy an authority or seek freedom in a new place. To strive for independence.

Blamavoidance. To avoid blame, ostracism, or punishment by inhibiting asocial or unconventional impulses. To be well-behaved and obey the law.

Counteraction. Proudly to refuse admission of defeat by restriving and retaliating. To select the hardest tasks. To defend one's honor in action.

Cognizance. To explore. To ask questions. To satisfy curiosity. To look, listen, inspect. To read and seek knowledge.

Construction. To organize and build.

Deference. To admire and willingly follow a superior. To cooperate with a leader. To serve gladly.

Defendance. To defend oneself against blame or belittlement. To justify one's actions. To offer extenuations, explanations, and excuses. To resist "probing."

Dominance. To influence or control others. To persuade, prohibit, dictate. To lead and direct. To restrain. To organize the behavior of a group.

Exhibition. To attract attention to one's person. To excite, amuse, stir, shock, thrill others. Self-dramatization.

Exposition. To point and demonstrate. To relate facts. To give information, explain, interpret, lecture.

Harmavoidance. To avoid pain, physical injury, illness, and death. To escape from a dangerous situation. To take precautionary measures.

Infavoidance. To avoid failure, shame, humiliation, ridicule. To refrain from attempting to do something that is beyond one's powers. To conceal a disfigurement.

Nurturance. To nourish, aid, or protect the helpless. To express sympathy. To "mother" a child.

Order. To arrange, organize, put away objects. To be tidy and clean. To be scrupulously precise.

Play. To relax, amuse oneself, seek diversion and entertainment. To "have fun," to play games. To laugh, joke, and be merry. To avoid serious tension.

Rejection. To snub, ignore, or exclude. To remain aloof and indifferent. To be discriminating.

Retention. To retain possession of things. To refuse to give or lend. To hoard. To be frugal, economical, and miserly.

Sentience. To seek and enjoy sensuous impressions.

Sex. To form and further an erotic relationship. To have sexual intercourse.

Succorance. To seek aid, protection, or sympathy. To cry for help. To plead for mercy. To adhere to an affectionate, nurturant parent. To be dependent.

Superiority. This need is considered to be a composite of achievement and recognition.

Understanding. To analyze experience, to abstract, to discriminate among concepts, to define relations, to synthesize ideas.

Although any list that attempts to cover the whole range of human needs will be incomplete, Murray's list is very helpful in determining what may be motivating someone in a particular situation. It also suggests areas for exploration when you are trying to influence someone. Because they do not relate necessarily to basic survival or other needs on Maslow's list, Murray's needs may be called *indirect* or *manifest*— needs that represent certain aspects or segments of a given motive or in some cases a combination of two or more motives.[3]

THE MOTIVATED SEQUENCE

Two other theorists, Monroe and Ehninger, use an adaptation of Murray's list to provide a framework strategy for making persuasive presentations. They call this strategy "Motive Appeals." Using motive appeals, Monroe and Ehninger show how certain combinations of manifest needs become powerful motivators. They begin by looking at the mental processes of a potential listener (or ally), who is the target of a persuasive message. They conclude that, despite the listener's individual

differences of temperament and ability, their thought processes in responding to various sorts of specific purposes are surprisingly uniform,
"so uniform, in fact, that they provide a practical basis for a standard
pattern of speech organization. We shall call this pattern the *motivated
sequence: a sequence of ideas which, by following the normal processes of human
thinking, motivates an audience to respond to the speaker's purpose.*"[4]

Monroe and Ehninger identify five distinct steps in the motivated sequence:

1. Attention
2. Need
3. Satisfaction
4. Visualization
5. Action

The steps in this sequence should be used as a tool for planning, and as
an organizational framework upon which to build the strategy for an
influential message. The steps, in application, will not be applied equally
in each instance. Sometimes one or more steps may be developed very
briefly, because the ally already understands that a need exists, or has
no objections to the satisfaction offered for the need.[5]

Table 7.1 is adapted from Monroe and Ehninger to pertain to the construction of an influential message.

PLANNING FOR STRATEGIC INFLUENCE

Two things are essential to be effective with strategic influence: knowing your subject, and knowing something about your ally. Personal information is always helpful, but while it is not critical to know a great
deal about the ally, it can be of help in establishing rapport and in determining what interests and motivates this person.

The main thing to know about a potential ally is what opinion he or
she currently holds with regard to what you want him or her to do.
During the give-and-take that accompanies an influencing encounter, it
is usually impossible to follow a fixed line of presentation. It is still very
helpful to be armed with a list of questions, usually of a fact-finding
nature, that will help uncover needs and other motivational elements,
like attitudes and beliefs. Fact-finding questions are those that begin with
phrases like

"How long have you been . . ."

"What has been your experience with . . ."

"Have you found satisfaction in . . ."

"If you could have it your way, how would you change . . ."

"Is there anything that bothers you about . . ."

Table 7.1
Construction of an Influential Message

Step	Function	Response
Attention, orientation, rapport building.	Getting attention, gaining control, building trust.	"I want to listen"; "I understand the issue"; "I like this person."
Identifying, or establishing need. Assess where person currently stands on the issue.	Describe and develop the problem under consideration. Motivate person to action.	"Something needs to be done [decided, felt]."
Satisfying need. Handling objections.	Present benefits of your point of view. Locate and satisfy secondary needs.	"This is what must be done [believed, felt] to satisfy the need[s]."
Visualizing. Summarizing.	Reiterate accepted benefits with visualization of results.	"I can see myself enjoying the satisfaction of doing [believing, feeling] this."
Action or closing.	Request tangible proof of acceptance.	"I will do [believe, feel] this."

The answers to the fact-finding questions will uncover needs and show you how the potential ally currently stands with regard to your position.

Wayne Minnick defined four situational strategies that cover the relationship between where a person is and where you want him or her to go.[6] He calls these

- The Goal Situation
- The Barrier Situation
- The Threat Situation
- The Identification Situation

To be effective with influence, an executive needs to determine in advance, or as quickly as possible, which of the situational strategies is appropriate for the individual subjected to the influence.

The Goal Situation

In a goal situation, the potential ally either already desires what you are offering or, it is assumed, will desire it once he or she comes to understand it. If, for example, you are looking for backing for the implementation of new accounting software, and a colleague walks into your office complaining about the amount of time it takes to get necessary numbers at the end of each quarter, you already know something very important about that colleague. He or she is goal-oriented.

To urge this person to achieve the goal, one may draw on some of the following ideas for questions and comments during the influential exchange:

1. The goal can produce benefits for the ally.
2. The goal is among the most significant or important goals the ally can seek.
3. The goal is deserved by the ally.
4. The goal is easily obtainable.
5. The goal is necessary for survival.
6. The goal will bring benefits to or is deserved by or is needed by those with whom the ally is identified.
7. The goal will bring long-lasting or permanent benefits.
8. Lesser persons do not seek the goal, but only those who are superior.

Influence, of course, runs both ways. If you want to convince someone not to achieve a certain goal, you would use basically the same approach stated in the negative, as shown in these statements:

1. The desire for the goal is unworthy of the ally; to seek it is irrational, unjust, contemptible; admirable people in the same situation have not been tempted by it.
2. The goal is unnecessary and would not meet a significant or worthy need or would not be long-lasting.

3. Other goals are more pressing, more possible to attain, more satisfying, more permanent.

4. The goal would be injurious rather than helpful or pleasant, or would produce benefits of a questionable nature, or is not what it appears to be.

The goal strategy assumes that an ally is already predisposed to the presented point of view or can be informed of the point of view in such a way as to create the desire for it. The emphasis in this strategy is placed on awareness, the attractiveness of the goal, and its accessibility.

The Barrier Situation

The barrier situation is the most common of the motivational situations. As Minnick puts it, "In a sense we are always separated from our goals, except at the instant of achieving them."[7] He lists some examples such as the following: a college student who wants a good mark but will not do the work; a man who wants the prestige of being a doctor but cannot get through medical school; the musician who will not practice; the athlete who will not train. In the barrier situation, the ally is also goal-oriented, but there is something that gets in the way of achievement. In order to urge the ally to overcome the barrier and achieve the goal, one may use some of the following ideas for questions and comments:

1. Increase the desire to get through, over, or around the barrier by increasing the desire for the goal.
2. The barrier is contemptible, unintelligent, unnecessary, or unjust.
3. The barrier works to the advantage of the enemies of the ally.
4. The person or circumstance that has raised the barrier has allowed others to achieve the goal that the ally actually deserves.

Again, the strategy can be reversed. To urge an ally not to surmount a barrier, use some of the following ideas:

1. Insist that the barrier is a necessary one.
2. Decrease the desire for surmounting the barrier.
3. Weaken the desire for the goal.

4. Request that the ally study the barrier more carefully. When action is delayed, the chances that the goal will be achieved are reduced substantially.

Although goal achievement is at the center of the barrier situation also, unlike the goal situation, the ally is both aware and desirous of achieving the goal but is hampered by some intervening factor.

The Threat Situation

Goal orientation also figures strongly in this situation. The difference is that the ally has already achieved certain goals. The threat is that they may be taken away. The emphasis here is on combating the threat. In order to urge an ally to resist and combat a threat, you may employ some of the following ideas for questions and comments:

1. The threat has the power to harm the prospect if not responded to promptly and powerfully.
2. Great effort can reduce the threat and has done so under similar circumstances.
3. The ally has the courage, power, and intelligence to resist the force.
4. Others less able than the ally have combated similar forces courageously and successfully.
5. The means, help, ideas, techniques, and other things necessary for combating the threat are at hand or will inevitably arrive.

Again, in the reverse situation, if you want someone to give in to a threat, shift the strategy in the opposite direction.

1. The threat is superior to the ally's power to resist and is close at hand.
2. Others, similar to the ally, have been defeated by the force although they expected to prevail.
3. Help is far away, the prospect is alone.
4. What the force attacks is not worth keeping.
5. Good sense requires that we give up the goal as others have done in similar circumstances.

To convince someone through threat, you must be certain that he or she has goals that are deemed worthy of retaining. You cannot threaten people who have nothing to lose.

The Identification Situation

Minnick describes the identification situation as one in which human beings become involved because they identify themselves with others. When we identify with a person or a group, their problems become our problems, their struggles become our struggles, and their failures and successes are experienced as if they happened to us. This situation is built on empathy. It is the same thing we experience when we are rooting for a favorite team. To motivate an ally to respond through identification, we must accomplish both of the following goals:

1. Convince the ally that the person or the group is in need, is facing difficulties not of his or her or their own making or fault.
2. Convince the ally that the person or group is like him or her in background, purpose, attitude, status, hopes, and the like.

This strategy is most often found in fund-raising or patriotic situations such as recruiting for the U.S. Army, Peace Corps, and Vista. As before, it can be reversed:

1. The source of the identification represents attitudes, values, and beliefs that are alien and hostile to the ally.
2. The need is not great, has been exaggerated, is their own fault, and they should be able to solve it alone.
3. Getting involved would expose the ally to danger, and the effort would be wasted.

Identification can be a powerful motivator, but it must continually be reinforced. It also works best when the ally is kept at a distance from the source of the identification so that you can control the perception of the similarities at the expense of the differences.

In summary, a main purpose at the outset of a strategic influence encounter is to determine where the ally stands with regard to your persuasive message. In this way the rapport-building phase becomes part of your strategic planning. In the give and take of the situation, motivation can shift. It is also probable, particularly in lengthy encounters, that more than one motivational situation will be evident. On a complex issue, the ally may be goal-oriented toward part of it, have a barrier to some of it, and feel threatened by still another part of it. The skillful influencer listens carefully and stays abreast of changes in motivation or uncovers additional needs or concerns.

THE POWER OF ACTIVE LISTENING

Since a major key to being effective with strategic influence is your ability to uncover the needs of the potential ally, your ability to listen effectively plays a major part. The art of listening is too often unappreciated, in part because listening is regarded as a passive activity. Some people believe that you can't show how much you know or illustrate your concern by listening. To the contrary, a person who is a good listener first will be much more effective when the time comes to present his or her ideas and concerns and ask for compliance.

Active listening not only helps you focus your attention on what the ally is saying; it can often go a long way to help the ally solve his or her own problems. Actively listening tells allies that you are interested in understanding what they have to say; that you care about them; and—amazingly enough—simply feeding back people's ideas often helps them sort out and come to the conclusion that you would like them to discover.

Active listening calls for sharing your understanding of what the person has said in such a way that he or she has the opportunity to clarify or confirm what you have heard. When you use active listening in this way, there are two things you will want to accomplish. The first is a restatement of the ally's thoughts. While it might seem unnecessary to restate something that has just been said, your playing it back demonstrates that you are listening, and it can often help the ally take a more objective look at what has been said. The second thing to accomplish goes beyond reflecting thoughts, and calls for the need to rephrase and reflect the person's thoughts and emotions in such a way that they appear consistent with previous behavior. Many of the factors in our model associated with intrinsic influencing are supported and enhanced by active listening behavior.

Barriers to Listening

It is discouraging to realize how many ways there are not to listen to other people. The fact is, it is impossible to listen all the time, for several reasons. Many of us spend as much as one-third of the time we are awake listening to verbal messages: from managers, co-workers, friends, family, total strangers, and customers. This means we often spend five hours or more a day listening to people talk. If you add this to the amount of time we tune in radio and television, you can see that it is impossible for us to keep our attention totally focused for this amount of time.

Another reason we find it difficult sometimes to listen carefully is that our personal concerns appear to be of more immediate importance to us than what other people are saying. Listening carefully is also difficult for psychological reasons. Although we are capable of understanding speech at rates of more than 300 words per minute, the average person speaks 100 to 140 words per minute. This leaves us with a lot of "spare time" to spend with our minds while the other person is talking. Current linguistic research indicates that most of us make up our mind what a word is going to be by the time we have heard the first consonant sound. The trick is to use this spare time to understand what the other person is saying better, rather than letting your attention wander: thinking about personal interests, daydreaming, or planning a response.

Here are some of the things that get in the way of being a good listener:

- The tendency to concentrate our attention on making a connection between what is being said and what we already believe.
- The tendency to judge or evaluate the content of what the other person is saying before fully understanding what we have heard.
- The tendency to jump to conclusions; hearing what we want to hear.
- The tendency to interpret words and phrases differently than the speaker intended (by-passing).
- The tendency to interrupt, preferring to hear our own voice over another's.
- Fear that we might have to admit we are wrong in what we assumed to be true about a person's needs.
- The tendency to feel we know more about what the person needs than he or she does.

It often appears that we have more to gain by talking than by listening. One big advantage of talking is that it gives you a chance to convince others of your point of view. In many situations it appears that the key to success is the ability to speak well. Certainly, when you are attempting to strategically influence somebody, sooner or later you are going to have to present effectively, and that requires talking.

Talking also provides the chance to release energy in a way that listening can't. When a person is frustrated, the chance to talk can often help him or her feel better. Talking provides a chance to gain attention and admiration. Tell jokes and people will think you are funny; offer advice and they will be grateful for your help. Tell them what you know, and they will be impressed with your wisdom.

While it is true that talking does have many advantages, it is important to realize that listening can pay big dividends when you are trying to get compliance from an ally. Listening provides a measure of control perhaps even greater than talking, since active listening demonstrates your willingness to hear others' concerns, and leaves them open to thinking about your ideas and issues. Listening is often reciprocal; you get what you give. It is a skill much like speaking; virtually everybody does it, though few people do it well.

Applying Active Listening Behaviors

There are four key behaviors associated with demonstrating active listening. These are:

1. Acknowledging
2. Sympathizing
3. Paraphrasing
4. Empathizing

Acknowledging demonstrates two elements of good listening. It shows that you are paying attention, and it indicates that you are hearing what is being said. It is the simplest of all forms of active listening, and can be done by verbal or nonverbal signs, which also function as prompts for additional information.

Acknowledging is a direct way to let allies know you are listening and receiving their message. It demonstrates interest and encourages the flow of information from the other person to you. Verbal and nonverbal acknowledging behavior says to your ally, "I'm listening. I might not agree or accept your point of view, but I care about what you're saying and I'm aware about what's going on."

It is very difficult to continuously attend to what another person is saying. At one time or another, we all lose track—especially in lengthy conversations. There is nothing abnormal about that; our ability to concentrate for a prolonged period of time is limited. When you find yourself tuning out, mirror back to the other person your best understanding of what has been said, even if it is wrong. That will provide the opportunity for the person to restate and/or clarify your understanding of what is being said.

One sure way to let people know you are paying attention is through eye contact. Reasonably consistent and natural eye contact is a sign of recognition and acknowledgment. When you look someone in the eye while you are listening to him or her you say, in effect, "I'm tuned in . . . I hear you."

Posture, and the movements of the body, can also affect a person's perception of the listener. If the listener is in continual motion, tapping a foot, fiddling with a pencil or a paper clip, drumming his or her fingers, and the like, others may get the impression that he or she is anxious to get on with it, which they may interpret as pressure. If, on the other hand, the listener focuses on them and nods affirmatively, people generally see that as acknowledgment.

Acknowledging verbally is particularly important when using the telephone. In the cellular phone world, we are all convinced when we haven't heard someone grunt or squeak on the other end of the line for a period of more than fifteen seconds, that they have gone into a tunnel and disappeared. But, even in person, it can be reassuring for the person you are talking to to hear some acknowledging noises just to reinforce that you are there and listening:

"I see . . ."
"Yes, go on . . ."
"Ah hah!"
"O.K."
"And then?"

Sympathizing sits at the next level of active listening. It demonstrates three elements of good listening: paying attention, hearing, and understanding. It not only acknowledges that the listener has heard what the person has said, it also reveals feelings about what was heard. Sympathy can run the gamut from pity and charity to sincere compassion for the other person's experience. When one sympathizes with someone, his or her feelings and concern are revealed. As a tool, sympathizing can be very helpful for the process of gaining and understanding other persons' feelings with regard to the issues and concerns you are raising. Allies will be more willing to discuss sensitive issues if they feel they are provided with a sympathetic ear. Sympathetic phrases can be very influential, because they focus on how you are feeling, rather than the other person.

"I am sorry that happened to you."

"That same thing happened to me, and I know what you're experiencing."

"I can appreciate why you're concerned about being short-handed."

As an influencing tool, sympathy involves sharing common feelings, interests, and loyalties. It appeals to altruism, esteem levels, and allurement.

Paraphrasing contains four elements of good listening: showing attention, hearing, understanding, and remembering. In fact, you need to listen very carefully to an ally's words if you are going to be able to restate, in your own words, your understanding of what has been said. It is doubly important if, for some reason, you have misunderstood what the person has said, since the process of paraphrasing provides an opportunity for the ally to correct, clarify, or amplify your understanding. To paraphrase effectively, simply put into your own words what you have heard. The goal is to serve as a verbal soundboard. Paraphrasing does not imply approval or disapproval of what has been said. It simply mirrors back your best understanding of what you heard.

"So what you're saying is that the incoming orders are outrunning production."

"If I understand you correctly, you would be interested in seeing some ideas that could help you provide better on-time delivery."

"Let me tell you what I'm hearing, Jack. You would like to set aside a certain amount of your budget in case there's a big push in the fourth quarter, so you don't want to use it up now."

It is important not to "parrot-phrase"—that is, to repeat back to the person exactly the words he or she said to you. This will appear trite and, in some cases, psychologically strange.

Empathizing is the most powerful act of listening skill. Like paraphrasing, it summarizes and reflects back to the ally the content of what he or she has been saying. However, it goes one step further and demonstrates your understanding of how that person is actually feeling. Understanding the concern, emotion, or motivational intent of what a person is saying is critical to understanding his or her inclinations.

Empathizing can be used very effectively to:

- Clarify feelings
- Demonstrate a sense of concern
- Increase your credibility
- Build additional trust
- Heighten the ally's enthusiasm for complying with your request

The key to empathy is to focus attention on the other person's opinion, concern, or feeling, and not your own feelings or opinions. For example, the phrase "I understand your concern" provides sympathy because it tells the other person how you feel. But the phrase "You are concerned about the future being uncertain at the company at this time" focuses on the concern from the other person's point of view. It uses the word "you" instead of "I" as the point of departure.

The use of empathy does not suggest or imply that you agree with the ally's perspective, but simply reflects your understanding of the concern. It also provides you with a springboard for tying your needs for compliance, wherever possible, to other factors that can promote influence—like demonstrating that complying with your request would be consistent with the ally's past behavior.

> "You feel that you haven't been steered in the right direction by the Marketing Department in the past."
>
> "You are concerned about how members of your staff will react if you add in this additional task."
>
> "You feel that, down the line, providing support for this initiative may come back to bite you if it doesn't work."

The goal of empathizing is to give the ally a clear indication of "This is my understanding of what you are saying and how you feel about it."

GETTING A COMMITMENT

We have a nearly obsessive desire to be, and appear, consistent with what we have already done. Having taken a stand, we are under a lot of pressure to maintain that stand and act in ways that are consistent with our initial position.

Research done at a race track illustrates this principle by looking at changes of behavior in people prior to betting on a horse and after betting on a horse. Apparently, after the bet was placed, people became more confident that their horse would win. This underscores the fact that, once a stand has been taken, the need for consistency pressures people to bring what they feel and believe into line with what they have already done.

Consistency as a trait is highly valued in the culture, and it is normally associated with personal and intellectual strength. Often people find themselves acting in ways that are contrary to their best interests, because on some level these actions appear to be consistent with previous behavior. In the strategic influencing process, the application of this tendency toward consistency is what I call the "Judo theory." The Judo theory asserts that requests for compliance or commitment are more likely to be successful if they are presented in a manner that coincides with previous or prevailing actions. If you have a good understanding of a potential ally's past behavior, and can identify consistent patterns of response, you can create a strong impetus toward gaining a commitment to comply with your requests—if those requests are positioned in such a way that responding favorably to them appears to be consistent with past responses the individual has made.

The entire act of compliance-gaining is essentially about getting someone else to commit to taking an action or a position that you are espousing. In strategic influence, commitment is sought and procured in stages. You begin looking for a commitment from the moment you begin the interaction. Begin by asking for the ally's approval to proceed. For example: "I have something I would like to talk to you about. Is this a good time?" If the person says "yes," you have received a commitment to procede.

You are also asking for commitment as you identify needs and concerns that relate to your issue. For example: "Would you agree that a change in the accounting policy would provide you with better data?" Here, again, if the response is "yes," the assumption can be made that the person has commited to the idea of change.

There is a further commitment associated with getting agreement that your solution, project, or concerns are worthy of his or her involvement. For example: "If we can get the new software up and running, we can probably produce those management reports before the next quarter. Would you agree that that would be good for both of us?" The commitment here relates to the person's willingness to make timing a priority.

Commitment is a two-way street. On your part, you are probably committing yourself to some action as well, particularly if the strategy you are using involves the exchange of currency. The ally is committing to providing the compliance that you are looking for. Certain things your ally may do or say will signal that he or she is ready to commit to your need for compliance. If you over-sell, you are in danger of talking them past the point where they were ready to commit. An experienced salesperson knows that the danger of "overselling" is the chance that additional objections may be unwittingly raised in the prospect's mind.

Commitment signals can be framed as questions or as positive statements relating to what you have proposed. For example:

"How much is this going to cost me?"

"What happens if we can't make the deadline?"

"Is this a one-time thing, or am I going to be stuck with it forever?"

Sometimes commitment signals appear as nonverbal responses on the part of the ally: nodding the head in a positive direction; sitting back and visibly relaxing; picking up a proposal or other material you have handed out and studying it. If you have been successful at controlling all the other elements of your influencing approach, the committing step should not be difficult. Think of all commitment as gaining permission to move on to the next possible step.

When a commitment to compliance is withheld, it is because the ally does not believe there is anything to gain from your proposal. Or, the ally may believe that the perceived risks associated with compliance outweigh the perceived benefits.

RISK ISSUES

Risk is a key element of every commitment decision. Although the concept of risk is most often in the context of investments, there is a broad range of psychological risk in all kinds of interpersonal transactions. A risk issue is any personal feeling an individual may have that results in his or her believing "I could lose something." Risk issues are not concrete, quantifiable, objective realities waiting to be tinkered with and fixed up by the savvy influencer. They cannot be overcome or talked around, like a reluctant buyer's objection.

A risk issue and an objection, although they may both impede your ability to influence, are two very different things. An objection is often the visible part of an underlying risk issue—or to put it in more scientific terms, the risk issue is the cause of the ally's reluctance, while the objection is the effect. When someone raises an objection, it could be a signal that some underlying reason is causing trouble. That something is a risk issue. Another difference between an objection and a risk issue is that an objection is usually tangible, and related to the factors involved in implementing your request. A risk issue is not. Risk issues are related to the individual's mental picture or concept about the relationship and, like any mental picture, they are generally intangible and personal.

Managing an objection, therefore, is very different from dealing with a risk issue. It is no less than the difference between cause and effect, and the most successful influencers are never content simply to deal with effects. They know that dealing with causes is fundamental, not only to getting commitment, but also to any long-term business relationship. Underlying risk issues that inhibit a person's ability or willingness to make a commitment to your proposal include, but are not limited to, the following.

The ally feels that complying with your request will create one or more of these feelings:

- Losing control
- Not being seen as a problem-solver
- Losing self-esteem
- Losing flexibility
- Being seen as a pessimist
- Being seen as a poor performer

- Losing leadership
- Losing credibility
- Being seen as "me, too"
- Incurring indebtedness
- Losing freedom of choice
- Being pigeon-holed
- Being put in a double bind (Catch 22)

Risk issues are specific to individuals; that is, they are highly personal. That is the fundamental point to remember about them, and it is why they are often difficult to determine.

Two related points bear some emphasis:

1. A risk issue cannot be judged. A risk issue is what someone is feeling deep down about what working with you will mean to him or her. There are ways to analyze and discuss and work with those feelings, but the one thing you should not do ever is to deny their validity. One of the surest ways to kill your opportunity to be influential is to say to someone with a risk issue, "You shouldn't be feeling that way."

2. Assumptions cannot be made about what the particular risk issue is, since the risk perception and non-commitment are always linked. It is safe to assume, when you cannot get commitment, that there is some risk issue involved—but it is hazardous to assume that you know what that risk issue is. It is easy for one risk issue to be confused with another.

Before you can identify a specific risk issue, you need to be able to recognize the underlying fact that a risk issue exists. You do that by watching for risk issue symptoms:

- Hesitation
- Skepticism
- Negative noises
- Aggressiveness or passive resistance

Symptoms arrange themselves into a hierarchy. As the symptoms escalate, the probability of a commitment diminishes. If you sense that your ally is merely hesitating, you still have time to identify and resolve the risk issue before the situation deteriorates. If the ally has become outright hostile, it is more difficult to continue attempting to gain compliance.

In some situations, if the risk issue is not resolved, your attempt to influence someone could turn into an argument. To prevent this, you need to ask risk-issue questions which will show how you stand and what still needs to be done to move the ally in the direction you want him or her to go. Asking risk-issue questions has a dual purpose. They help you understand your ally's reasons for feeling the situation is a "lose" for them. On the other hand, they help you uncover what still needs to be done to turn the situation around. Following are some examples of risk-issue questions:

"Michael, I'm getting the impression that committing yourself to meeting with my task force once a month is making you uncomfortable. Can we talk about that?"

"Donna, it's really important that you believe in what we're doing. Are you getting the sense that, by cooperating with my department, you would be losing control over some of the areas for which you have responsibility?"

"I think I need to back up and provide some additional explanation of what I'm trying to do here. You seem to feel that you're being locked in. Is that right?"

"Jim, you seem to be skeptical. Is there something I should know that you're not telling me?"

You also use this kind of question as a final test of your ally's commitment. For example:

"John, I'm feeling good about what we've decided, but you're the one who has to live with it. How are you feeling right now?"

"Mary, are you comfortable that you understand what I need from you, and all the issues that surround it?"

When you ask an ally for commitment, there are at least four possible responses:

- "Yes."
- A qualified yes ("Yes, but . . .")
- An objection/obstacle ("I'm still concerned about the . . .")
- A flat "No."

In each of these four situations, an appropriate response on your part is critical to either turning the situation around or at least preserving an ongoing relationship.

1. If you receive a firm "Yes," the logical and appropriate next step is to thank the ally, reinforce the decision, and terminate the interaction.

2. If you received a qualified "Yes, but . . ." you need to identify the ally's reservations or concerns. Very often an ally is responding with a qualified "Yes" because he or she is simply seeking some additional information, looking for some additional reassurance, or offering a relatively minor objection which may need clarification.

3. If you receive an objection, it is important to process this objection in the way that has helped you be successful to this point. Before attempting to answer an objection, it is important to question and actively listen to understand exactly what the concern is. Handled poorly, you risk raising additional objections.

4. If you receive a flat "No," this should be a sign to you that you have not done as good a job as you could have in tying your need for compliance to some need or consistency factor for the ally. It could also represent a defensive reaction; your ally may simply be resistant to the notion of compliance in general. It may have nothing to do with you. Perhaps the ally has been burned in the past by associating him- or herself with a similar request. This circumstance then becomes a risk-issue situation, and you may be able to retrieve the potential for compliance by asking risk-issue questions.

Regardless of what other factors may enter into the influencing dynamic, sooner or later you will find yourself having to present your position, point of view, need, or concern to a potential ally. How you strategize that presentation will go a long way toward determining how effective you will be in meeting your objectives.

NOTES

1. E. C. Tolman, "The Determiners of Behavior at a Choice Point," *Psychological Review* 45 (1938): 1–41.

2. Abraham H. Maslow, *Motivation and Personality* (New York: Harper & Row, 1954), 80–106. Also see Abraham H. Maslow, "A Theory of Human Motivation," *Psychological Review* 50 (1943): 370–396. Finally, see Abraham H. Maslow, "Some Theoretical Consequences of Basic Need Gratifications," *Journal of Personality* 16 (1948): 402–416.

3. H. A. Murray, *Explorations in Personality* (New York: Oxford University Press, 1938), 127.

4. Allan H. Monroe and Douglas Ehninger, *Principles and Types of Speech* (Glenview, IL: Scott, Foresman, 1967), 265.

5. A broader discussion of the weighting of the various parts of the motivated sequence can be found in Marvin Gottlieb, *Interview* (New York: Longman, 1986).

6. Wayne C. Minnick, *The Art of Persuasion* (Boston: Houghton Mifflin, 1957), 84.

7. Ibid.

CHAPTER 8

Influencing Despite Authority

Let's face it. There are some organizations in which the hierarchy exists—
and where you are on the hierarchy still makes a difference. As a manager or supervisor, with people reporting to you, there are still
opportunities to simply order people around. In fact, there may be many
times when that is precisely what is called for.

However, when dealing with today's survivor populations, before
managers can lead effectively or motivate, they must first define and
understand their own significant role in the achievement of the various
business objectives. The evidence, however, seems to suggest that for the
long term there are much more productive approaches than simply giving orders.

An interesting dichotomy is presented by younger, better-educated
jobholders who, while having become distrustful of the organizations
they work for, in fact express a very strong work ethic.

> More than seven out of ten jobholders surveyed who endorse the
> new cultural values also subscribe to a strong work ethic. They feel
> an inner need to do the best job possible, regardless of pay. We are
> left with the following questions then: If workers have an inner
> need to give their best to their jobs, and if increasingly they have
> a great deal of control over their level of effort on the job, what is
> preventing them from giving more to their work? Why do they

hold back, and what steps can be taken to encourage them to give more?[1]

A significant part of the answers to these questions lies in the type of relationship the manager establishes with subordinates. A study done by Dansereau, Graen, and Haga identified two types of relationships. One they call leadership (in-group); the other supervisory (out-group). The determination of which type of leadership is taking place is based on the content and character of the exchanges that managers have with subordinates.[2]

According to this perspective, leader-member exchanges are distinguished by the quality of the resources exchanged by the two parties. Due to limits on time and other resources, and to differences among members, leaders do not distribute resources uniformly. In leadership exchanges, supervisors invest considerable assistance, attention, support, and informal rewards, and grant subordinates (in-group members) considerable latitude in negotiating their roles.

In such exchanges, supervisors and managers influence their employees without recourse to formal authority, and provide opportunities for reciprocal influence.[3] On the other hand, with out-group members, the supervisor's investment is limited to the behavior specified in the organization's formal or contractual definition of authority relationships. Managers in such exchanges exploit role-prescribed authority to gain subordinate (out-group) members' compliance. In-group subordinates are apparently more likely to share their supervisors' perceptions of significant work problems, are more satisfied, are less likely to leave the organization, and are better performers. What this suggests quite overtly is that, given the general climate of the workplace and the character of today's survivor workplace populations, the most successful managers will be those who cultivate the leadership-type exchanges. Further, to the degree that managers are successful in cultivating these relationships, they will also position themselves to be more influential.

In a study by Vincent Waldron, tactics used by subordinates in order to develop and maintain relationships with their supervisors were studied. Among other findings, Waldron confirmed that in-group subordinates seemed to have freedom to communicate with their supervisors outside of formally prescribed channels, about issues not directly related to their work. Further, the study found that this latitude was not available to out-group members.

In-group subordinates apparently have freedom to communicate with their supervisors outside of formally prescribed channels about issues not directly related to their work—a kind of latitude not available to out-group members. Such informal communication may result in a supervisor who is better informed about the subordinate, more knowledgeable about the circumstances influencing the subordinate's performance, and more inclined to develop friendship ties with the subordinate.[4]

The study further found that in-group members also conformed to organizational expectations, and assisted the supervisor in obtaining the compliance of other employees. They share higher levels of loyalty to the supervisor and the organization. In summary, the members of the group subjected to the leadership model displayed positive attitudes in response to supervisor task assignments, clarifying expectations, and conforming with work rules.

All of the evidence seems to support the development and maintenance of informal networks, not only among peers and superiors, or people outside of the organization, but also with those people who are assigned to report to you. Influencing subordinates becomes relatively easier when you have presented a clear vision and when those with whom you operate on a daily basis support that vision. Some managers can create their vision and direction from within themselves, and then develop support for it. Others work with their subordinates to create a vision together.

It is having a clear vision that will allow you to align and direct the energy and resources of your subordinates to achieve your desired goals. Communicating your vision to your team helps them define their roles and direction. When roles and responsibilities are clear, it is easier for you to exert influence to gain the necessary compliance you are looking for.

It is up to the executive to initiate the creation or refinement of the vision and mission. Time needs to be set aside to meet formally on the issue, without neglecting the informal channels. Working with the team, strategies should be identified for achieving the goals that are collectively set and to identify the critical success factors necessary to accomplish them. Periodically there is a need to re-examine the vision and mission to ensure that it is on target, and that everyone is still on board. Again, the informal network channels are going to provide the most reliable information.

In the current business environment, roles and responsibilities appear to be in constant flux. The manager needs to continually assess and re-negotiate role responsibilities. Entering into this process with your team also provides opportunities for a more generalized team-building experience. From my point of view, it is preferable to have several short meetings rather than one long one, assuming that the short meetings are frequent and focused. Try to find uninterrupted time for your team to meet. Also, it is often effective to use an outside facilitator, preferably a professional, when feelings are high or issues are complex.

A better understanding of roles and expectations can be facilitated by having the individuals on the team describe what they would like others to do more of or less of as the case may be. On an individual basis, during performance reviews, a manager can help set goals and clarify each person's contributions to the overall success of your efforts. The idea is that today's successful manager is not focusing on making people work, but rather on creating a climate within which workers willingly provide the organization with a large measure of their discretionary effort.

The relationship side of management outweighs the substantive side in large measure. Even in situations where people are connected at a distance electronically, and are heavily responsible for their own results, there is a need—whenever possible—to interact face-to-face as much as possible with all the people who are directly involved in accomplishing the work that the manager is responsible for. It is this direct contact, both formally and informally, that fuels your ability to influence the people who work for you to provide that extra measure of discretionary effort. It is easy to be (or at least appear to be) influential when all of the decisions that need to be made are benign—that is, they do not create risk issues for any of the people involved, including yourself. However, we all know that this is usually not the case. Today's managers are frequently faced with circumstances that call for courses of action that, in their aftermath, raise complaints, breed additional problems, and garner negative reactions. If you are to gain and retain influence with the people who report to you, you must be perceived as someone who takes these possibly difficult actions openly and courageously.

Here is a list of behaviors that you can engage in that will maintain your ability to influence intrinsically:

• Support your people, particularly when they are under attack from outside from above.

- Confront the tough issues.
- Don't be tentative. When "no" is the answer, say "no."
- Examine your own resistance to change.
- Stand up to your management. Not only will that make you more influential with your own direct reports, but most upper-level managers will also respond favorably.
- Don't fight every battle. Be selective about where you expend your energy. As much as possible, involve your direct reports in the hard issues by directly soliciting their input and support. If your people come to you with problems, let them know exactly what you plan to do. Avoid being vague.
- Deal with your people problems when they occur. You will lose the respect of your peers and your direct reports if you are not willing to deal with people who are negatively affecting the team's success or morale.
- Be consistent. Work against any tendency to second-guess yourself. Stay with yourself once you have made a decision, and avoid reopening the decision-making process unless compelling information is brought to bear.
- Ensure that your direct reports receive the responsibility and accolades for their own good decisions and behaviors. If you are like most managers, you do not have a completely clear perception of how you are coming across to others.

I always recommend engaging in some sort of a 360-degree assessment that will provide you with in-depth feedback about your leadership style, the areas in which you need to improve, how you interact with people, and specific management competencies like coaching, giving orders, delegating, handling crises, communicating, and so forth.

THE INFLUENTIAL COACH

Perhaps nothing the manager does is as important, or in some cases as difficult, as providing necessary support and counseling to subordinates. Coaching and counseling situations present a challenge and a test of the manager's resources and skill. The fact that influence is an integral part of coaching is almost a non-sequitur.

Certainly all of the various elements of our influencing model come to bear in the coaching situation—the intrinsic factors, the extrinsic factors, and the strategic factors. However, in most instances of influence that we have already discussed, you enter into an influential dynamic because you need some sort of compliance from another party. In the coaching and counseling construct, the primary goal is for one participant to help the other, and the lines are clearly drawn. The person being counseled is at the center. He or she is all-important, and everything else is incidental. That person may have sought us out, or have been forced by someone or something to seek our counsel. The problem for a manager in this scenario is to find out how to best help this person, who may even resist or resent the attempt.

The key word is "help." What does "help" mean in this context? Alfred Benjamin, in *The Helping Interview*, grapples with this issue:

> I am not certain I can define "help" satisfactorily to myself. . . . Help is an enabling act. The interviewer enables the interviewee to recognize, to feel, to know, to decide, to choose whether to change. This enabling act demands giving on the part of the interviewer. He must give of his time, his capacity to listen and understand, his skill, his knowledge, his interest—part of himself. If this giving can be perceived by the interviewee, the enabling act will involve receiving. The interviewee will receive the help in a way possible for him to receive it as meaningful to him. The helping interview is the largely verbal interaction between interviewer and interviewee in which this enabling act takes place. It takes place but does not always succeed in its purpose; often we do not know if it has or not.[5]

For those of us who do not engage in counseling as a profession or on a regular basis, it is useful to see this type of interaction as an enabling act. This gives us the right mindset when the situation does occur. What can we do to enable the counseling to take place in the most effective manner? Certainly the setting is essential. Also, monitoring our own communication at each major step of the process—especially with regard to the questions we ask and the responses we make—will provide us with a framework within which we can exert the necessary influence.

Aside from the influencing aspect, coaching is an essential part of good management. It is difficult for people reporting to you to improve their performance if they don't know their strengths or when the performance needs improvement. Effective coaching can be quick, frequent, and informal, or thorough-structured and in depth. It can also be done one-on-

one or in small groups. Whatever the situation, there are skills and guidelines that can help you become a more effective coach for all your direct reports, and in those situations outside of the immediate organization where you are called upon to play this role. One of the first mistakes that managers make with regard to coaching is the assumption that a particular action that is useful to help one individual will be the same for a wide range of situations or a wide variety of individuals.

A man walking down the street is approached by a stranger, who asks if he knows where Main Street is. The man points it out to the stranger and says, "Straight down and to your left." Assured that he has been understood, the man walks on—but he notices that the stranger is walking in the wrong direction. "Sir," he says, "you're going in the wrong direction." "I know," replies the stranger, "I'm not ready to go to Main Street yet." As individuals, we are unique, and what we discover is that we can best help others by enabling them to do what they themselves really want to do. The stranger had asked the man for directions. The man had given directions to the best of his ability. The stranger had understood, but was not ready to go in the direction in which he was pointed.

Sometimes we want to move others too quickly along the path. At what point are we interfering, or are neither wanted nor needed? The best coaches know that influencing people to move in a certain direction, or to help themselves, often does not take place in a rapid cause-and-effect relationship. A coach is only half of the equation; the other person involved needs to take a large measure of responsibility for what happens.

Coaching sessions occur for two reasons; because they are initiated by the subordinate or because they are initiated by the manager. Experience tells us that most coaching sessions are initiated by the manager. However, this is not an absolute, and in fact many opportunities for coaching are lost because the manager did not identify the subordinate's request or concern as a potential coaching opportunity. When a subordinate asks to see you, the most sensible thing to do is to let him or her state what led to the need for the meeting. This is not always easy to do. You may feel that you should know what the issue is, and let the person know, so you might say, "So, I guess you're having problems with your report." This may or may not be correct. If it is, you gain nothing except, perhaps, a sense of pride in guessing right. If it is not correct, the subordinate may be put in an awkward position. He or she may feel that this is what the meeting should be about, and so—not wishing to contradict—may agree, even though the real issue was something else entirely.

A better approach is to let him or her state why the meeting was requested. After the formalities of greeting and being seated, the most useful thing you can do is listen as hard as possible to what the person has to say. If you must say something, it ought to be brief and neutral:

"Please tell me what you wanted to see me about."

"I'm glad we have this chance to talk."

"I understand you wanted to see me."

"What's on your mind?"

Here are some basic things to remember about the coaching session:

- The subordinate does not always know what help may be available.
- The subordinate may know, but not be immediately able to verbalize it.
- The subordinate may know, but hesitate to state it bluntly so soon.
- The subordinate may not like the idea of having to come for help.

Avoid using the words "help" or "problem" when initiating a coaching session. Don't open with, "What problem would you like to discuss?" The subordinate may not have a problem, or may not have thought of it as a problem until you said it. The word "problem" is a heavy word, that used at the beginning, out of context, and without knowing how the subordinate reacts to the word, could potentially hinder rather than help a coaching session. Perhaps the key point to remember is that this person has come to you for a specific reason—that he or she has a genuine interest in this meeting, and as long as you do not get in the way, he or she will begin to talk.

When initiating a coaching session, move directly to orienting the person to what the meeting is about. State at the outset exactly why you asked the subordinate to come and see you. For example:

"I've gone over the report on your projected budget for the fourth quarter, and I wanted you to come in so that we can talk over some of the areas where your group seems to be having difficulty."

"You've been working with Sally and observing her for about three weeks now, and I've asked you to drop in to see me so that we can talk about your impression of the job and how you feel about moving into that area."

"By this particular point in time, we find that many of our most successful salespeople have developed a fairly substantial list of leads. You seem to be falling a bit behind the pace, and I wanted you to come in so that we could discuss it."

The great danger in the manager-initiated session is the possibility that it will turn into a monologue, a lecture, or a combination of the two. This danger can be avoided if you stop talking after indicating what the purpose of the coaching session will be, and have furnished the information, if any, you intended to give. Subordinates will usually have a great deal to say if they feel you are ready and willing to listen to them. Avoid putting your subordinate on the spot by saying such things as:

"I suppose you know why I've asked you to come in."

"We both know why you're here."

"Can you guess why I asked you go stop by?"

These openings are usually perceived as threatening. Subordinates may not know, and yet fear that you won't believe they don't know. They may think they know, and not wish to tell, or they may imagine several reasons why you asked them to come in and become confused. This approach may be perceived as a challenge, and reacted to in kind. Depending on their style, some subordinates may decide to resist rather than cooperate. In short, it is very doubtful that this sort of opening will bring two people together.

The person being coached is entitled to know immediately your purpose in calling him or her in for a discussion. The more honest and open you are, the more honest and open the other party can be. You need to demonstrate at the outset that your purpose is to provide assistance, and not make judgments.

Demonstrating Interest and Concern

The intrinsic influencing element of trust is a critical factor in the success of any coaching session. One way of enhancing this trust, and demonstrating interest, is to ask questions. These initial questions must be open-ended, friendly, and non-threatening. Plan and practice your questions so that they are natural and effective. Your subordinates will judge you by your skill at asking perceptive questions and the sincerity and thoroughness of your answers.

Another way of building trust is self-disclosure. Self-disclosure is any revelation about yourself that is not readily apparent through observation or prior knowledge. Self-disclosure should not be irrelevant or too intimate. Used with care and discretion, self-disclosure can be an effective tool for establishing rapport and encouraging the exchange of information. For example, you might say: "Let's see. This is the way I was feeling after my first six months."

Too many personal war stories can have the opposite effect, or—as my son used to say, when I would launch into what I thought was an important trust-building self-disclosure, "Dad, is this going to be another one of your 'when-I-was-a-boy' stories?" That aside, responses to relevant self-disclosures are usually positive. This happens because when you reveal information about yourself you appear trustworthy. Self-disclosure also encourages others to disclose, and reduces the initial defensiveness in a new relationship.

Demonstrating interest and concern may be a distinctly separate element, or integrated with the greeting. It can range from non-related personal comments to asking a subordinate about his or her interest in the company. The purpose is to indicate that you are interested in that individual as a person as well as an employee. When interest and concern have been exchanged, both you and the subordinate will more easily discuss the issues at hand. Expressions of interest and concern tend to build trust, and trust is a key component for stimulating the free flow of information.

Prelude to Coaching

Following are some things to think about or prepare for prior to engaging in a coaching meeting.

1. Coaching, to be effective, should be an ongoing process, not a rare and isolated event. Coaching should be expected and accepted as an ongoing part of the routine.

2. Coaching sessions should be conducted in a reasonably private environment, so that others in the immediate area are not aware of the specific feedback you may be providing. Praise in public; criticize in private.

3. Let the subordinate know that you are going to be conducting a coaching session. When you schedule a session to discuss the feedback, you should let the person know what performance you will be using as a basis for your feedback.

4. Before you can coach a person to improve, he or she must have a clear understanding of your goals and an opportunity to perform. Without goals and baseline performance measures, coaching becomes subjective and general.

5. Accurate feedback about how an employee is performing, based on specific goals and standards, is the essence of the coaching session. Use assessments to help you coach toward standardized proficiency goals and provide accurate baseline performance data for your discussion with your employees.

6. Always try to arrange a coaching session with as positive an expectation as possible. "I'd like to discuss with you some of the ways that will make you more effective on the telephone. I also want to point out some things that you are doing very well."

Recognize that you are a part of the coaching environment. Ask yourself a couple of questions:

- How do I feel about being a coach?
- How do I feel about coaching this particular individual?
- What would I like the outcome to be?
- What do I anticipate the outcome will be?
- If there is a discrepancy between my expected and desired outcomes, what would be the causes for that?
- How do I think the other person feels about being coached?

- What can I do to make this coaching session as helpful to this person as possible?

External Conditions

External conditions such as the room where the coaching session takes place are difficult to specify, since they are a matter both of individual taste and of the limitations dictated by the spaces available in the existing offices. Of course, a coaching session can be carried out almost anywhere, and it would be preferable, for other external reasons, that it occur in a room. The room can be any room you normally use for work, as long as the atmosphere is not threatening, noisy, or distracting. The person being coached will adjust to this.

Under ordinary circumstances, nothing that is part of a manager's usual work material needs to be hidden away. You will probably want to put aside files on other employees in your charge, customer files, the remains of a late lunch, or any other items that would detract from the professional atmosphere of the room.

The question of how to arrange chairs often arises. In most coaching sessions, no more than two people are involved, and usually you decide where you and the employee will sit. There is no definitive answer as to right-or-wrong arrangements. Some managers like to sit behind a desk facing the employee. Others feel best when facing the employee without a desk between them. Still others prefer two equally comfortable chairs placed close to each other at a 90-degree angle with a small table nearby. This is a matter of personal style, and you most probably already understand what arrangement you are most comfortable with.

A coaching session is personal, and deserves and needs the respect you wish to show the employee. Once you appreciate this fact, you will find a way to achieve the necessary cooperation from your associates. In this chapter, I have attempted to provide an overview of the problems and solutions associate with being influential when you have power. The following chapter looks into specific influencing objectives for the coaching process.

NOTES

1. Marvin R. Gottlieb and Lori Conkling, *Managing the Workplace Survivors: Organizational Downsizing and the Commitment Gap* (Westport, CT: Quorum Books, 1995).

2. F. Dansereau, G. Graen, and W. J. Haga, "A Vertical Dyad Linkage Approach to Leadership within Formal Organizations: A Longitudinal Investigation of the Role-Making Process," *Organizational Behavior and Human Performance* 13 (1975): 46–78.

3. Ibid.

4. Vincent R. Waldron, "Achieving Communication Goals in Superior-Subordinate Relationships: the Multi-Functionality of Upward Maintenance Tactics," *Communication Monographs* 58 (September 1991): 301.

5. Alfred Benjamin, *The Helping Interview* (Boston: Houghton Mifflin, 1969), ix–x.

CHAPTER 9

Influencing Job Performance

Perhaps the most immediate and ongoing influencing situation for managers is that of influencing for enhanced or continued job performance. Traditionally, this process is called coaching. The coaching dynamic is complex; it drifts between the boundaries of command, control, discipline, praise, and blame. The focus here is on the part that influencing plays and the skills needed to make coaching effective.

QUESTIONING TO IDENTIFY NEEDS

The most important tool for a coach is the questions he or she asks. The best coaches are those who ask questions rather than make presentations—those who listen more than they talk. Your success as a coach depends on knowing your people. Questions are your means of collecting information about what the person you are coaching really needs. Without them, the manager is dependent on assumptions and whatever information the person is willing to volunteer. In addition, questions are the means of controlling the conversation. This is because questions have a very powerful influence on the other person's behavior.

The following checklist is adapted from *Managing the Workplace Survivors*. It highlights potential problems.[1] If your questioning behavior is not adequate:

- Did you help the employee open up his or her perception of the problem as much as possible?
- Was he or she able to look at things the way they appear to him or her, rather than the way they seem to you or someone else?
- Was the employee free to look squarely at what he or she sees as the concern and to express it, or did he or she perceive the concern through the eyes of someone else?
- Did the employee find his or her own problem, or find a problem he or she thought should be found?
- Did your attitude or approach prevent the employee from exploring his or her own experience, unhampered by external influences?
- Did you help the employee move toward action and away from inaction with regard to his or her needs?
- Did you help the employee explore and express what he or she found as a need, rather than respond to your preconceived idea about what the need is?
- Did you let the employee tell you how he or she genuinely feels about a problem, or how things truly look to him or her?
- Did you let the employee explore his or her concerns in his or her own way, or did you lead him or her in a direction you chose?
- Did your behavior truly indicate the absence of threat?
- Did you really want to listen to the employee, or did you want the employee to listen to you because you already had the answer to the problem, because you were anxious to scold or correct, or because you really did not want to hear anything you did not know how to manage?

BEFORE BEGINNING A COACHING SESSION

Coaching, to be effective, should be an ongoing process, not a rare and isolated event. Your ability to influence depends on the relationships you have established. This is the same for your direct reports as it is for anyone else in the organization.

The coaching sessions should be conducted in a reasonably private environment, so that others in the immediate area are not aware of the specific feedback being provided. Again, praise in public; criticize in private.

While some sessions are spontaneous, where possible the person should be informed that this is going to be a coaching session. When one schedules a session to discuss the feedback, the subordinate should be told what performance will be used as a basis for the feedback. Before a person can be coached to improve, he or she must have a clear understanding of the manager's goals, and an opportunity to perform. Because of their proximity, the manager should have strong ties with his or her direct reports. This translates into shared values and goals. Without goals and baseline performance, coaching becomes subjective and general. Accurate feedback about how a person is performing, based on specific goals and standards, is the essence of the coaching session. Always try to arrange a coaching session with as positive an expectation as possible. "I'd like to discuss with you some ways that will make you more effective on the telephone. I also want to point out some things that you are doing very well."

Ask yourself these questions:

- How do I feel about being a coach?
- How do I feel about coaching this particular individual?
- What influencing strategies are appropriate for this person?
- What would I like the outcome to be?
- What do I anticipate the outcome will be?
- If there is a discrepancy between my expected and desired outcomes, what would be the causes for that?
- How do I think the other person feels about being coached?
- What can I do to make this coaching session as helpful to this person as possible?
- Have I been successful at influencing change in this person before?

INTRINSIC INFLUENCING BEHAVIOR

There are three primary internal conditions that are relevant to the successful coaching session:

1. Being ourselves—desiring to help.
2. Knowing ourselves—trusting our ideas.
3. Being honest—listening and absorbing.

Two internal conditions are basic to the desire to help:

- Bringing to the coaching process just as much of your own knowledge, skill, and personal experience as is needed, stopping at the point where this may hinder the process or deny the person the help he or she needs.

- Feeling within yourself that you wish to help this person as much as possible and that there is nothing at the moment more important to us.

If one is at ease in the role of a coach, he or she will be in a better position to understand the other person during the coaching session. This ability to focus on the other person will help the other person develop trust. If the coach does not feel the need to hide behind a mask, the person being coached will, in turn, hide less. The more the coach can be free from a preoccupation with his or her own behavior, the better he or she will be able to concentrate wholeheartedly on the person being coached: listening to understand, trying to find out what it is like to feel the way the other person does, and demonstrating a genuine interest in the other person's problems.

Of course, as the boss, you are expected to have ideas, suggestions, and solutions of your own. Because of the relative positions of authority and the tendency of subordinates to accept your point of view in such situations, you must present your ideas as expressions of opinion that are not binding (except in cases where they are policy). The person being coached should feel that he or she will continue to receive the manager's respect, no matter how he or she responds to the expressed feelings and ideas.

Ideally, the employee will arrive at a plan of action that enables him or her to accept both the responsibility and ownership of the result and, at the same time, is acceptable to the manager. While this is the ideal, it often becomes necessary for the coach, particularly in performance-problem situations, to be more assertive about the necessary actions toward a solution. However, sometimes managers are so concerned with what *they* are going to say next that they find it difficult to listen to and absorb what is going on. In the coaching situation, what the boss has to say is generally much less important than he or she thinks it is. Enthusiasm for one's own ideas should not get in the way. It is the other person who needs the help. The manager does not need to prove how confident he or she is.

PLANNING

Timing for coaching is an important element. To be most effective, the coaching session should be timed to occur very close to the performance the manager wants to coach. If too much time passes between the behavior and the coaching session, important, specific information may be lost. In conducting a coaching session, there are some general points to keep in mind from the beginning. These points form the basis of the coaching plan.[2]

1. *Prepare for the session* by writing down some specific—even if rough—notes and an outline or agenda. The more specific you can be, the more helpful your feedback will be. Preferably, the individual whose progress or performance you will be discussing will be able to prepare some notes or discussion items from his or her perspective as well.

2. *Create a positive environment.* Use some ingratiation. During the session, try to remain as positive and optimistic as possible regarding the individual's ability to improve the performance you plan to work on. Confidence and positive expectations are important to a person's motivation to improve.

3. *Specific observations are critical to good coaching.* Do not attempt to identify every "glitch" in the individual's performance. Rather, focus on the most significant aspect or two which can be improved. Write down the issues you will focus on before the meeting rather than trying to do it while one or the other of you is talking.

4. *Avoid personality issues or generalizing performance.* A criticism such as "You really don't seem to care," all by itself, is not very helpful. The words or data you use to draw that conclusion are important. You will be able to discuss the information openly with the individual if you have set a positive environment and have made clear that your interest is in helping him or her to improve.

5. *Avoid setting yourself up as the perfect example of adaptability.* To be an effective coach does not require that you be better than each

person. It does require that you be perceived as wanting to help, having valid observations, and being able to offer good ideas for improvement.

6. *Demonstrate good coaching skills* throughout the coaching session. For example, you should not interrogate an individual with a series of closed-ended questions and then tell him or her that he or she needs to ask more open-ended questions. Rather, you should probe and ask open-ended coaching questions which cause the individual to gain insight into his or her performance and other concerns.

7. *Demonstrate your understanding of the individual's point of view* by empathizing—summarizing both the facts and feelings that he or she provides. It is an excellent way to build both trust and rapport. You should look for opportunities to describe appropriate benefits for him or her as a result of improving performance based on your coaching suggestions.

8. *Close on commitments* at the end of the coaching session. This is critical to confirming your, as well as the individual's, understanding of what is expected as a result of the coaching session. This also involves an exchange of currencies. What are you willing to do in order to facilitate the desired change of the other's behavior?

Throughout the process, the manager is highlighting intrinsic influencing factors: trust, concern, understanding, and the like. He or she is communicating to the employee that both parties understand the facts of his or her situation, and can articulate the associated feelings.

Once this understanding has been achieved, you now have come to the point in the coaching session where the boss and the subordinate have to get down to cases. That is, it's time to move toward a plan of action that is going to resolve what is perceived as a coaching issue.

USING PERSONAL EXPERIENCE

While there are many things to do at this stage, our discussion of responding begins with a few don'ts:

- Don't respond to every concern raised by the other person with an example from your own personal experience.

- Don't interrupt or feel the need to fill all silences.
- Don't use the phrase "If I were you, I would . . ."
- Don't say, "I know just how you feel."
- Don't use the word "why" unless you are seeking limited factual information.

Of course, the executive's personal experience is a valuable asset, and there will be a place in the coaching session where that personal experience and the associated anecdotes will be invaluable. Because of the manager's greater experience, the temptation to use personal example during the coaching session will be almost irresistible. Personal experience, or the examples presented, hold meaning for the manager. They do not necessarily hold meaning for others. War stories may make the employee hesitate to express how he or she honestly feels about a situation for fear of offending, or because the experience he or she is describing varies from the example the manager is providing. He or she may think, "Well, perhaps that worked for you, but if I were you, I'd be sitting where you are now and not be in this mess." Also, because you are the manager, the employee denies him- or herself freedom of expression and may appear to accept what you have said and cause you to believe that you have been of help when you have not.

The best time to use experience and examples is when they are solicited. At that point, an introductory phrase such as "This has worked for me, but I can't say whether it will work for you," or "This helped me, but I wonder how you feel about it" will set the stage for a response to your example non-defensively.

The key, as always, is to work hard at keeping the lines of communication open. This is why phrases like "If I were you, I would . . ." create problems for the coaching session. The employee might be thinking, "If you were me, you'd feel just as confused and unsure as I do," or "If you were me, you wouldn't know what to do any more than I do." A better response in this circumstance is to come straight out with "I think your best bet at this point is to . . ." or "I feel that, right now, the wisest thing you can do is . . ." since these responses at least sound sincere.

Insincerity is a trust-buster. That's why a phrase like "I know just how you feel" creates problems. The employee could be thinking, "How can you know how I feel? And if you know, so what?" If one genuinely feels what the employee is feeling, that has probably already been expressed through the listening behavior.

THE PROBLEM WITH "WHY"

Perhaps the single most frequently used word in the process of asking questions is "why." A good coach is sensitive to many things, but perhaps a sensitivity to the use of the word "why" is what separates really excellent coaches from also-rans. "Why" has so often been misused that its original meaning has become distorted. It was once a word used to search for information; it signified the investigation of a cause or reason. When used this way, it is still appropriate, and there is no other word that does the job as well. Unfortunately this is not generally the way it is used. The word "why" has come to connote disapproval or displeasure. When it is used by a manager, it implies that the employee has done something wrong, or has acted in a manner that is unacceptable, even when that is not the meaning you intend. The word "why," used in the coaching context, invariably raises defensiveness.

Young children use the word frequently. It enables them to explore and discover. They ask for information without implying moral judgment, approval, or disapproval. However, in time they learn that adults use the word differently. "Why," spoken by an adult, puts children on the spot and shows them that they are behaving in an unacceptable manner: "Why did you muddy the floor?" "Why are you barefoot?" "Why don't you use your knife and fork properly?" "Why did you break that dish?" The child learns to imitate this behavior, and pretty soon will say to a friend, "Why did you take my bike?" to show that he disapproves of the act and not because he or she is interested in obtaining a bit of useful information, or "Why must I go to the store?" not because he or she wants a reason, but because he or she doesn't want to go. At the same time children learn this use of the word "why," they discover a way to defend themselves. They will answer, "Because." Whenever people hear the word "why," they interpret it as meaning "Change your behavior. Act the way I want you to act." And they respond accordingly.

Regardless of your intention, "why" is often perceived as "Don't do that" or "I consider this bad" or "You ought to be ashamed." As a result, the employee will defensively withdraw, attack, or rationalize, but will not feel free to explore or examine the situation at hand. Because of your authority, you may extract an answer to the question "why," but more likely than not it will be one that has been produced to satisfy you—one the employee feels you want to hear, rather than a true, significant step forward for the employee in his or her understanding of the problem.

With some thought and effort, the same questions can be asked without using the word "why." Here are a few examples:

"I've noticed that you haven't yet completed your report, and I'm wondering if there's something I might be able to do to help you."

"One thing we've discovered over the years is that there's a direct relationship between a salesperson's success and the ability to respond directly to prospects' questions, so product knowledge is very important. Can we talk about where you currently stand with the product materials I gave you?"

THE THREE-STEP RESPONSE PATTERN

It is important to note at the outset that each coaching situation is unique. Two individuals, given the same circumstances, will not respond in precisely the same way. Therefore, the pattern of response suggested here is best viewed as a topographical map—a good indicator of the terrain leading toward your objective, but not one that restricts you to only a single path.

Hopefully, by this point in the coaching session, good rapport and a feeling of trust have been established. Defensiveness is minimized and the employee has been oriented to the coaching process as the manager intends it for this session. Some open-ended questions have been asked, followed up with probes, and the manager feels at this point that he or she has a reasonably good understanding of the general feelings and concerns. It is now time to move the session toward some agreed-upon plan of action.

Step One: Reinforce

Make a positive statement. It is very important at this stage in the process to keep defensiveness at a minimum. One way to do this is to reassure the employee that you are aware of the positive things that are happening, as well as your concerns. Reinforcing positive behavior at this stage will keep the dialogue open. Indicate which skills or behaviors you have observed are being performed well. Make sure that this positive reinforcement is done in enough detail so that the employee will know how to repeat the behavior in future situations.

"Your productivity has really picked up over the last few months. Those additional prospecting calls are really paying off."

"You did a fine job of closing on the Johnson sale. I know they were considering one of our competitors, and it's through the excellent relationship that you were able to build that you got that sale."

"I received some very good feedback from one of your clients on how responsive you were to their questions when they spoke with you on the phone last week."

"I want to tell you that you've come a long way with the product knowledge. You really sound as though you know what you're talking about."

"I want to tell you that, at a recent meeting, I used your example of how to handle the increase in cost, and everyone was very impressed."

"I think that one of your key advantages that will figure very strongly in your success is your ability to stay cool under fire."

Having provided positive feedback, wait for a response. Allow the person whatever time he or she wants to take to discuss the point, expand on the issue, or simply enjoy your praise.

Step Two: State Concerns

Express your concern about an area needing improvement, or highlight the next desirable development stage. How you respond at this point in the process depends on the nature of the coaching session. If the object of this meeting is further development, at this point you will want to discuss what you feel would be the next logical step, or your vision of the future progress required during the short term. In either case, it is often a good idea to ask the employee to analyze his or her performance before you comment in detail. One of your primary goals as a coach is to help your people learn how to evaluate and improve their own performance. Asking them to analyze their own performance will reinforce the fact that this is a behavior they should be engaging in throughout their career, and especially when you are not there. Also, it provides an opportunity for you to learn how effective the employee is at analyzing his or her own problems.

Sometimes there will be disagreement about your perception of his or her performance. When this occurs, you can help the employee to perceive a development need, or strength, by using a few closed-ended questions focusing on the specific issue.

"Do you remember the objectives we set at our last meeting?"

"Do you remember how the Jackson delivery was held up because the transmittal was not completed in the proper way?"

If the coaching session centers on a performance problem, you will express your perception of the problem as a "concern." The word "problem" is too loaded, and puts up defensive guards.

"I'm concerned that your project is behind schedule. What can I do to help you move it along?"

"Your productivity seems to be down the last couple of months. What can we do to get your numbers back up there where they should be?"

"There have been some complaints from the staff that you have been difficult to get along with. This concerns me. Are you stressed about something? What can we do to fix it?"

"I'm concerned that you seem to have difficulty answering questions on the new benefits package. What do we need to do to get you up to speed?"

"My sense is that, during the planning meeting, there was an opportunity to support our project, and I'm wondering why you didn't go for it?"

Step Three: Develop a Solution

Evaluate and modify the employee's suggestions into something you can agree to as a plan of action. As a coach, the manager must always keep in mind that the person closest to the problem is often the person closest to the solution. In addition, when someone comes up with his or her own plan of action, the level of commitment is much higher. If the employee is unable or unwilling to provide an acceptable plan of action to improve performance deficiencies, it could be because of a lack of experience, or an inability to cite what the deficiencies are. In this case, the manager will need to suggest a way to modify or develop the particular skill being coached. In other instances, the employee may suggest a plan of action which from your point of view is inadequate. Be prepared to provide better options for developing the particular skill or behavior being coached.

It is important, during this step, to elicit feedback to make sure that the employee knows what you expect. Ask questions that require an explanation. Do not ask: "Do you get it now?" "Are we clear on this?" "Can I depend on you to do that better?" Instead, ask: "Tell me what you're going to do the next time this situation arises." "Explain to me in your own words what you think I want you to do."

Finally, summarize your understanding of what has been agreed to:

> "All right, so we're agreed that you will spend two hours a day for the next two weeks studying the training materials. Then you will take the appropriate certification tests and I will keep track of your scores."

> "OK. At nine o'clock next Monday morning, you and I will meet here and role-play the call before we go at ten o'clock."

> "So you feel we need more frequent contact, and I agree. For the next month, I'm putting it on my calendar that we will meet every Monday morning."

Much of your influence will depend on your making commitments and keeping them.

COACHING OPPORTUNITIES AND APPLICATIONS

Having appropriate and effective coaching behaviors at your disposal is only part of the equation. Which behaviors the manager selects and how he or she applies them will be determined by the context of the coaching situation (see Figure 9.1).

To some extent, each coaching session is unique because the individuals involved in the process are unique. However, it is possible to group various approaches under distinct headings according to the need for the coaching session:

- Coaching for a change in general behavior
- Coaching for specific job improvement

- Coaching the average performer

- Coaching to manage the entrepreneur

- Coaching the star performer

Figure 9.1
A Coaching Model

---

1. **Initiating and Planning**
   - Identify specific issues for coaching.
   - Plan strategy, make list of questions.

---

2. **Questioning**
   - Get information about the:
     - —Person.
     - —Activities.
     - —Goals.
     - —Obstacles.

---

3. **Actively Listening**
   - Clarify and confirm understanding of content and feelings by:
     - —Acknowledging.
     - —Sympathizing.
     - —Paraphrasing.
     - —Empathizing.

---

4. **Responding and Resolving**
   - Provide support for positive performance.
   - State specific concerns or observations and ask for input.
   - Evaluate and modify suggestions into a plan of action.
   - Address and resolve objections, obstacles, or uncertainties through:
     - —Questioning.
     - —Actively listening.
     - —Responding with ideas and suggestions.
     - —Confirming understanding and acceptance.

---

5. **Committing to Action**
   - Summarize action plan for both Agent and Manager.
   - Ask for and confirm commitment to accomplish goals of the plan.
   - Express confidence in the outcome and provide a solid statement of support.

STRATEGIC EMPHASIS

Let's begin with an overview of the complete blueprint for the coaching process.

Initiating Contact and Planning

- Initiate dialogue.
- Demonstrate interest in the employee and his or her problem by establishing rapport, creating trust, and building a level of comfort.
- Orient the employee to the coaching session and gain control of the situation.

Questioning to Identify Employees' Needs

- Ask questions about the person, their actions, their goals, and their understanding of your goals, and the obstacles that interfere with their ability to achieve those goals.
- Ask open-ended questions to obtain more information, especially early in discussion.
- Ask closed-ended questions to clarify and confirm information.
- Look for both factual and feeling information.
- Use follow-up or probing questions to gain further understanding.

Active Listening

- Acknowledge (give verbal or nonverbal signs that you have understood) to demonstrate interest and encourage the flow of information.
- Sympathize (make comments like "I understand . . .") to demonstrate your concern.
- Paraphrase (reflect back the content) to assure the employee that you have heard and understood.

- Empathize (reflect back feelings and content) to build trust and relationship. (Make comments like, "You must be very frustrated that deliveries are consistently late.")

Responding with Solutions and Resolving Concern

- Make a positive statement and restate the need you are about to discuss based on information you received from your questioning.
- Express your concern about an area needing improvement or highlight the next desirable development stage for the employee and ask for suggestions.
- Evaluate and modify the employee's suggestions into a plan of action, and summarize your understanding of what has been agreed to.
- Question to clarify the specific nature of any objection or concern.
- Actively listen to demonstrate understanding of the employee's point of view.
- Respond with appropriate suggestions.
- Confirm acceptance by direct questions on the acceptability of the resolution. (Ask questions like "Does this cover your concern?" or "Can we agree that this approach makes sense?")

Committing to Action

- Summarize the employee's needs as you understand them.
- Ask the employee to summarize the actions agreed upon.
- Ask the employee to confirm his or her commitment to the agreed-upon actions.
- Provide a solid statement of support.

Remember, being criticized is not a comfortable situation for most of us. Even when it is well-meaning and constructive, the fact that you are coaching the employee about a performance issue suggests that he or she has failed in some way. It is extremely important, at the end of each coaching session, that you make a statement that reinforces your belief in the future success of that employee.

"I feel very good about the solutions we've come up with. If we can both keep our ends of the bargain we're going to do very well getting you up to speed. You are potentially a top member of this team, and I believe you can succeed. Now, let's do it."

"Despite the fact that we have a little ways to go, I don't want you to take these criticisms as an indication that you are not doing well. Everyone starting out has areas that need improving. I believe in you, and I know you're going to make it."

Each of the following coaching concerns requires a somewhat different emphasis, although the skills involved in initiating questioning, listening, responding, and closing are necessary in each case.

COACHING FOR A CHANGE IN GENERAL BEHAVIOR

Preparation for Coaching

Undesirable behavior may or may not affect employees' productivity. People can be effective workers but unpleasant to deal with as colleagues and subordinates. They may not present themselves in a way acceptable to the professional standard set by your organization. There may be some ethical concerns. The key to identifying this type of coaching problem is to ask, "Is the behavior I want to change related to specific job skills, or to the more general way the person presents him- or herself?"

In preparation for coaching a change in behavior, ask yourself these questions:

- What is the behavior needing change? Try to state this in as specific terms as possible.
- How has the behavior come to your attention? Was it through personal observation, or the observation and subsequent report of others?
- Is the employee aware of this behavior?
- Does the employee perceive that the behavior provides rewards, such as higher productivity, greater recognition, and the like?

The next step in your preparation is to consider what actions are available to you. Does the behavior warrant disciplinary action? If disciplinary action is called for, are you prepared to apply it consistently and follow up to ensure that it is effective? Would the advantages of disciplinary action be offset by the negative effect of one side against the other? In most cases, you will determine that trying to discipline a particular behavior change will not be as effective as finding alternative ways of meeting the employee's needs that are more acceptable to everyone concerned.

Strategic Application

Strategy for changing behavior focuses on the questioning and responding portions of the coaching blueprint. As much as possible, you must learn the reasons for the person's behavior. Any behavior, particularly when it is not clearly associated with primary job performance issues, will be strongly defended by an employee who may interpret your concern as a personal attack. The behavior might be satisfying a psychological or social need that you are not aware of.

To minimize the possibility of a defensive response that will inhibit the coaching process, the manager continues to ask open-ended questions and look for opportunities to empathize with the employee's experience. Once the cause of the behavior has been identified, and understanding of the need for the behavior expressed, the manager can make a transition to a suggestion for an alternative behavior that may satisfy the same need. In some instances the employee is not aware of the behavior. Therefore, an awareness question is always useful early in the process.

Manager: George, I've called you three times this week, and I wonder if you're aware that you sound very curt and abrupt in our discussions. Is there a problem that I'm not aware of?

Employee: I wasn't aware I was coming across that way. However, all three times you called me were at ten after nine, and I was involved in trying to get my schedule ready for the day. I don't mean to be abrupt; it's just not a good time for me to talk on the phone.

Manager: You're saying that you would like a little extra time in the morning to get your act together before you have to deal with me.

Employee: That would be great. Call me at ten, and you'll find a different person.

Sometimes, however, the employee is aware of the behavior, but feels that it helps him or her meet a particular need. Again, the manager's strategic emphasis is on questioning and responding. One caution, as noted earlier in the text: avoid using the word "Why" in the questioning process, as it enhances defensiveness:

"Why are you snapping at people?"

"Why do you dress like that?"

"Why can't you straighten up your office?"

A better way to get at the same issues might be:

"Is there something going on with you that I'm not aware of? I've noticed that you seem to be somewhat short-tempered these days."

"I'd like to go over some of the factors that seem to make a difference in the success of a management consultant. We have found the way an associate presents him- or herself to be very important. If you were a client, how would you expect a consultant to look?"

"George, I know they say a cluttered desk is the sign of a creative mind, but I'm wondering—could you use a little help getting your office organized?"

In the best of circumstances, the employee will respond with suggestions that lead toward a commitment to an alternative behavior. However, any direct suggestions that you make should be very clear about:

- What behavior is acceptable as an alternative.
- What the negative behavior is doing to the individual and possibly to others as well.
- How the employee's needs can be met through other, more positive behaviors.
- How in some cases the employee's needs cannot be met at this time, and why.

As in all cases, when behavior change is desired the manager must find positive things to offset the criticism and be particularly sensitive to the need for ending the session with a solid statement of support.

COACHING FOR SPECIFIC JOB IMPROVEMENT

Preparation for Coaching

Performance deficiencies may arise from a variety of factors. Finding out what may be causing the need for performance improvement is important, because it sets the tone of the coaching session. If the concern is with a new recruit with performance problems, that situation will not be handled the same as with a veteran who has suddenly developed a performance problem. The key to identifying the proper approach is to ask what the underlying cause of the performance problem is. In preparation for coaching for specific performance improvement, ask yourself these questions:

- What is the performance problem that needs addressing? Try to state this in as specific terms as possible.
- How has the performance problem come to your attention? Was it through personal observation or the observation and subsequent report of others? Was it based on productivity numbers? and so on.
- Is the employee aware of this behavior?
- Has he or she received the latest reports, brought the issue to your attention, or changed his or her normal pattern of behavior?
- Is there an external reason why performance is not meeting expectations, such as change in assignment, additional projects, general business conditions, and so forth?

The next step in preparation is to consider what actions are available. Is this a first time discussion regarding this performance issue, or is this a constant or recurring problem that may require a warning or disciplinary action?

Strategic Application

Strategy for specific performance improvement focuses on the questioning, resolving, and closing portions of the coaching blueprint. Open-ended and follow-up questions need to be used to ensure an understanding of the problem from the employee's point of view. Getting quality feedback from the employee is extremely important for the performance improvement strategy.

When one becomes aware of a performance problem, it must be addressed as soon as possible. Delay in dealing with the issue can create problems down the line. Keep in mind that, if the intent is to be influential rather than disciplinary, the objective is to provide guidance for future performance, not to make judgments on past mistakes.

> *Manager*: Louis, I want to talk to you because we need to discover what's causing you to make errors in your end-of-day settlements. Monday your total was over; Wednesday you were short. Today you're short again. Do you have any thoughts on what's happening?
>
> *Employee*: I think the problem comes from being constantly interrupted while I'm tallying the drawer. I'm the last teller to close, so customers keep coming in while I'm counting.
>
> *Manager*: But the late customers go on the next day's tally.
>
> *Employee*: I know, but if I don't start counting by 2:45, I can't get out of here in time to catch my train.
>
> *Manager*: What do you think we can do about it?
>
> *Employee*: Well, if we had another teller working, I could stay with the count.
>
> *Manager*: Let's try this: I'll have Julie do her count early and then take your window for the last fifteen minutes. That way, you can finish your count and go over your numbers before you turn them in.
>
> *Employee*: That would work.
>
> *Manager*: OK, Louis, we'll try that today. I'll talk to Julie and set it up. Let's meet again next week and see how it's going. Louis, you have been very conscientious and I like the way you deal with customers. Let's put this counting problem behind us.

Resolving becomes important in this coaching process because the performance problem most likely is related to something the employee either doesn't understand, is uncertain about, or sees as an obstacle to achievement. Criticism should be constructive. Find what is good about the performance and stress those aspects first.

Immediate job-related and detailed discussion concerning the performance problem will produce an action plan that can dramatically improve performance in the short term. A performance issue usually requires that the manager make commitments as well. Therefore, in the closing portion of the coaching session the manager needs to summarize an action plan for both him- or herself and the employee that clearly states:

- the obligations for improvement.
- the means to achieve the necessary support to be provided to ensure the success of the plan.

As in all cases, when being critical of performance, positive things to offset the criticism must be found, and a statement of support provided.

COACHING THE AVERAGE PERFORMER

Preparation for Coaching

The first problem with coaching an average performer is making a determination of what the term "average" means. If a manager uses only productivity figures to determine performance, he or she will fall into a trap. Some performers fluctuate from high to low performance over a period of time, and the net result appears to be average. Other performers are consistently average, but the results of both performers appear to be the same. In fact, the employee whose performance fluctuates should be coached for a performance problem. The employee who has consistently average performance is targeted in this session. The key to identifying the type of coaching called for in this situation is to ask what is causing average performance for this employee, and what might be the optimal capability of this employee.

In preparation for coaching the average performer, the manager asks these questions:

- What constitutes average performance for my team?
- What constitutes superior performance for my team?
- Have I communicated my standards and expectations clearly and directly to the employee in question?

- Could the employee's average performance be based on a lack of knowledge and skill, rather than on a lack of the necessary motivation to excel?

- Does the average performance represent the consistent level for this employee, or a change from past superior performance?

- Is the employee aware that his or her performance is considered average?

- Is the employee a relatively new recruit or a veteran who seems to be slipping?

The next step in preparation is to consider what actions are available. Average performance rarely calls for disciplinary action. Sometimes, although it is hard to accept, an average performer will remain average despite your best efforts. In this case, the manager must make the judgment that perhaps the coaching efforts are better placed elsewhere.

Strategic Application

Strategy for coaching an average performer focuses on the initiating, questioning, and responding portions of the coaching blueprint. How you initiate this session can strongly influence the outcome. An opening like: "Jane, I called this meeting because you're not cutting it. I'd like to find out what you're doing wrong" will immediately raise defensive barriers that will be difficult to remove. Instead, initiate a session this way:

Manager: Jane, I've called this meeting because I've always felt strongly about your capacity to succeed. My sense is that something may be holding you back. I'd like to work with you to see if there are some opportunities that we are missing to get your output power to a higher level.

As in all cases, questioning is important to determine why the performance is average, or why the performance fluctuates. In some instances, the answers you discover may be a surprise to both of you. Failure to excel may not be a motivational issue, but rather the result of lack of knowledge, skill, feedback, or direction.

When responding to the employee's problems and needs, the manager presents ideas, suggestions, and actions that are clearly understood and within the ability of the employee to perform. Often an average performer is not a new recruit, but a veteran. Almost inevitably, the result of average performance for the veteran is drifting away from using the basics. Time might be spent going over old production reports from when the employee was performing far above average, and illustrating what was going on at that time to support that excellent performance.

Whether dealing with a veteran who has slipped or a relatively new recruit who is not progressing, the manager must put across in the coaching session:

- His or her belief in the employee's ability to achieve excellent performance.
- What is considered to be excellent performance.
- His or her willingness to be involved in any agreed-upon action that will move the employee from the current plateau.

As in all cases, when a negative judgment about performance is unavoidable, it is important to end the session with a solid statement of support.

COACHING TO MANAGE THE ENTREPRENEUR

Preparation for Coaching

Most managers have obviously experienced success in their work behavior. They have come up through a tradition that presents tried-and-true methods for achieving individual business goals. There is always a temptation to think that their way is the only way. In fact, in most instances, the existing approaches will yield the best results. However, as changes occur in the marketplace and workplace, it is important for managers to be open and to give innovation a fair test rather than rejecting it out of hand. After all, the only way in which improvements in procedures and methods occur is through innovation.

Employees may attempt innovative approaches out of frustration or excitement with a new idea. Attempts at innovation are often unsuccessful. Coaches have to distinguish between the employee's intent for the innovation and the end result. If a manager reacts negatively to an innovative attempt, he or she sends a message to the employee to avoid trying new things.

In preparation for coaching to manage innovative behavior, a manager should ask these questions:

- Who initiated the coaching session? You will react differently if an employee requests a meeting to "run an idea by you" than if you perceive an unusual behavior and call him or her in to discuss it.
- How did the innovative behavior come to your attention? Was it through personal observation, or the observation and subsequent report of others?
- Is the employee aware that this particular behavior differs from the norm?
- What is your best guess as to why the employee might be trying this behavior?

As with other coaching situations, the next step in preparation is to consider what actions are available. Remember, it is easier to manage or control an innovative performer than to stimulate innovative behavior from a complacent and cynical team.

Strategic Application

Strategy for managing innovation focuses on the questioning and active listening portions of the coaching blueprint. Perhaps above and beyond any other issue associated with this type of coaching, the manager must discover the intent behind the innovative behavior—that is, why did the employee feel it necessary to try this particular action? When the results of innovative behavior are negative, there is a natural tendency to reject the behavior out of hand. There is a need to identify the intent behind the action.

Manager: John, it seems to me that you are trying something new with the shipping process. Could you help me understand what you are getting at?

Also, if the innovative behavior had negative results, there is a need to determine whether these results were caused by errors in judgment or a lack of knowledge, or because there is a difference between the goal the manager thought was being attempted and the one actually being attempted.

For all these reasons, active listening is very important. Paraphrase and empathize, as appropriate, to ensure understanding of the employee's intent. In the process of doing this, the manager will also send a strong message that he or she is very interested in learning what motivated the innovative action. Even if the results of an attempt at innovative behavior were negative, there is a need to indicate support for the well-meaning attempt at innovation.

> *Manager*: So, what you're saying, June, is that by telling the customer that your manager insists that you get at least three referred leads, you felt that he would feel sympathy for you and be more willing to provide you with names?
>
> *Employee*: That's right.
>
> *Manager*: You are feeling frustrated at not being able to get a substantial number of referred leads from your recent sales presentations.
>
> *Employee*: Yes.
>
> *Manager*: June, as we all know, referred leads are our best source of prospects. I commend you for trying to gather more of them, but I'm not sure this approach is working. Let's work it through and see if other options might be available that will get you better results.

A rational influencing strategy often works with this person. In the presenting of ideas and suggestions, the focus should be on the thinking process that created the innovative behavior. Develop ideas and suggestions that demonstrate a connection between the employee's idea and the idea or suggestion the manager is going to make. Choose phrases like:

> "If we make a modification on this approach . . ."
>
> "There may be additional benefits if we . . ."
>
> "Let's consider the possibility of a different approach to this problem . . ."
>
> "I see what you're trying to accomplish. Here is a way we might be able to achieve what you're looking for . . ."

It is important that the employee "buys in" to the suggested modifications. Therefore, as manager you should be very clear about:

- Stating your understanding of the problem.
- Why the innovation concerns you.
- What the results of using the innovation in its current form on a continual basis may be.
- How your alternative suggestions fit with the original intent.

The statement of support at the close of the coaching session should underline the fact that innovative behavior is a good thing, and that the employee will continue to be valued for such behavior, even if it doesn't always work.

COACHING THE STAR PERFORMER

Preparation for Coaching

Obviously this is a coaching problem all managers should have more of. The reason why coaching the superior performer is a problem does not derive from the difficulties associated with coaching this type of individual, but rather from the likelihood that such an individual will *not* receive coaching.

Superior performance tends to be credited by the manager when it appears, and rapidly becomes taken for granted as you turn your attention to what appear to be more pressing problems. The old adage "If it ain't broke, don't fix it" does not apply here. Coaching good performance makes it occur more frequently; if it is ignored, it tends to occur less frequently. The superior performer may have areas of insecurity or problems he or she is unwilling to bring up for fear of lowering your high opinion.

In preparation for coaching the superior performer, ask these questions:

- What behavior or behaviors require praise?
- Where have you seen improvement, even within the context of superior performance?

- How did the employee's superior performance come to your attention? By direct personal observation? By the observation and subsequent report of others? Or both?
- Is the employee aware that he or she is a superior performer?
- Does the employee currently feel that he or she is receiving enough recognition and reward as a consequence of superior performance?

The next step in your preparation is to consider which behavior you are going to praise. Superior performers should be praised often, but not for everything. Also, as with all behavior change, the praise should be provided as soon as possible after the superior performance has occurred.

Strategic Application

The strategy for coaching the superior performer focuses on the initiating and closing portions of the coaching blueprint. Make it very clear at the outset that you are speaking with the employee because you want to provide praise. "Sally, I am so pleased I was able to go with you to that meeting this morning, and that I have the opportunity to tell you how well I thought it went."

Managers need to work against a natural tendency to be detailed in criticism and abrupt with praise. For example, "Jack, I think there are six or seven reasons why you are having difficulty with that data base. Let's go over each one of them. First of all . . ." or "Judy, great job." An effective coaching session for a superior performer provides very specific itemized observations of what is being perceived as excellent behavior.

Sometimes people find it difficult to receive praise, primarily because they are not used to getting it. Be sure to leave enough time during the session for the employee to respond in whatever way he or she feels appropriate. It is during those moments that problems and difficulties which have not previously surfaced may appear, since the employee feels secure in your respect and has a high level of trust. Remember at the end, even though the entire coaching session was punctuated with praise, you still need to provide a solid statement of support.

Coaching from an influencing perspective is a collaborative act. The goal is the same as with all influence attempts: to gain compliance. All three modes of influence come into play when coaching for performance.

The intrinsic influencers focus on the relationship with the employee. The extrinsic influencers focus on what the manager can offer or exchange for compliance. The strategic influencers shape the presentation of the manager's point of view.

NOTES

1. Adapted from Marvin R. Gottlieb and Lori Conkling, *Managing the Workplace Survivors: Organizational Downsizing and the Commitment Gap* (Westport, CT: Quorum Books, 1995), 164.

2. Ibid., 163.

CHAPTER 10

Influencing Up

O! sir, content you;
I follow him to serve my turn upon him;
We cannot all be masters, nor all masters
Cannot be truly follow'd. You shall mark
Many a duteous and knee-crooking knave,
That, doting on his own obsequious bondage,
Wears out his time, much like his master's ass,
For nought but provender, and when he's old, cashier'd;
Whip me such honest knaves. Others there are
Who, trimm'd in forms and visages of duty,
Keep yet their hearts attending on themselves,
And, throwing but shows of service on their lords,
Do well thrive by them, and when they have lined their coats
Do themselves homage: these fellows have some soul;
And such a one do I profess myself.

Iago in *Othello*, Act I, Scene 1

Sometimes the notion of influencing the boss gets a bad rap. Iago is a bad role model. He conjures up images of dishonest manipulation leading to large measures of destruction and human suffering. On the other hand, there is a little of Iago in all of us. That is, we engage in influencing upward for something more than altruistic reasons. If we are bucking for promotion, for example, there is a large measure of self-interest included in our package of motives. While we probably don't wish any ill upon our superior, often we are less concerned about his or her welfare than we are our own.

Despite the self-interest issues, there are many other reasons why upward communication and its associated influence are important in today's organization. Many studies have documented how communication is often distorted when it is aimed in an upward direction. There are many reasons for this, including the fear of "shooting the messenger." During a consulting assignment for a large travel and tourism company, I listened in amazement while the then president of the company bragged about high morale and company loyalty, when I knew that employees were preparing to leave en masse and were stealing the pictures off the walls.

On the other hand, many companies can point to successes based on the encouragement from the culture for upward communication. Harley Davidson again comes to mind and the super-successful retailer Walmart. Sam Walton has been quoted as saying that the best ideas come from clerks and stock boys.[1]

Upward communication conveys a variety of messages:

- Progress reports and general activity
- Issues, problems, obstacles, triumphs, and opportunities
- Ideas, solutions, innovations
- General morale, interpersonal conflicts, information form the informal network

When one is in the position to communicate any of these things to a superior, he or she also has an opportunity to be influential. Managers at every level should be seeking out this type of information on a regular and continuing basis. On the simplest level, receiving communication from subordinates provides feedback on how the downward communication is being received and dealt with. The reasons for upward communication are compelling and obvious enough not to be enumerated here. As a result the climate within which communication with superiors takes place should be improving along lines of openness and honesty. However, many subordinates find communication with a superior stressful and difficult despite the advantages to both the individual and the organization.

There is much to be gained by opening up to the boss, but there is also a perceived risk. Telling the boss you dislike your current assignment could get you another assignment. It can also get you fired. This fear of being punished for communicating honestly in an upward direction inhibits not only the communication but also the opportunities to engage in influencing behavior. Most managers can readily assess how their superior will receive various types of communication. Once assessed, an appropriate strategy can be developed for contacting that superior at a level acceptable to him or her. It would be preferable if the superior created opportunities for regular interaction and communication; but, barring that, it is the subordinate's obligation to try to make it happen.

Looking at the research, and addressing the issue of superior-subordinate relationships, a few things become apparent. First, most of the studies conducted in this regard focus on the relationship between supervisors and line workers. Relatively few investigations have been conducted that examine a manager's relationship with his or her superior. Secondly, while many of the assumptions and discoveries concerning supervisor-subordinate relationships are applicable to influencing up from the manager's perspective, there are some significant differences.

One assumption that probably holds true for managers is the relative stability of a relationship with the superior once it is established. While the reasons for establishing and maintaining a good relationship with an organizational superior are obvious, they break down into a few subcategories. Some subordinates seek nothing less than a close friendship with the superior. For others, maintenance of an appropriate level of professional respect is sufficient. In those cases where a manager dislikes his or her superior, the objective might be simply to preserve a sense of civility and politeness and to avoid as much overt conflict as possible.

Waldron and Krone conducted a study of emotional communication at work. Their findings show that some subordinates who had experienced extremely negative emotional encounters with their superiors altered their definition of the relationship from "friends" to "co-workers" and edited their communication to make it more formal, superficial, task-oriented, and devoid of personal messages. Despite those changes, those subordinates were often careful to maintain regular contact with their superior, and to avoid emotional outbursts. The conclusion was that it was apparent, even under extreme conditions, that subordinates are unlikely to allow complete degradation of the important leader-member relationship.[2]

Some researchers have stated that in organizational settings, maintenance of an acceptable relationship with a supervisor may be the most critical communication objective, as employee socialization and advancement are largely dependent on successful achievement of this goal. Obviously this is increasingly important, depending on where the manager falls in the hierarchy of the organization. Supervisors and middle managers most probably have greater concern for the maintenance of this relationship, due to the potential for advancement, than do executives much closer to the high end of the hierarchy. Also, it appears that subordinates who have historically worked hard at developing and maintaining optimal relationships with their superiors fare much better when personal relational and organizational goals conflict. Superiors tend to be less threatened by upward influence attempts, more sympathetic to excuses for performance failures, and more supportive of subordinate protests over relationship or organizational injustices when a good ongoing relationship has been established with a subordinate.

Waldron conducted another study to determine what tactics subordinates used to maintain their supervisory relationships. While the group he studied included both blue- and white-collar workers, the results appear to be applicable for a person at any level trying to maintain and establish a good working relationship with his or her superior. Four factors emerged as being associated with influencing up.

- Personal factors
- Contractual factors
- Regulative factors
- Direct factors[3]

PERSONAL FACTOR

Personal factors describe attempts to initiate or encourage informal communication with a superior. The items included in this factor suggest that frequency of interaction and emphasis on personal content, rather than job-related content, are the defining features. In general, these personal factor items suggest that informal communication is used to build and maintain the friendship ties with the superior. The items included in this factor are:

- Talk with him or her frequently, even when I have nothing important to discuss.

- Ask about his or her personal life.
- Frequently engage him or her in small talk.
- Share jokes or amusing stories.
- Treat him or her like a friend.
- Make a point to interact with superior at social gatherings.
- Compliment the superior frequently.
- Talk about past experiences we have shared.
- Encourage the superior to discuss the problems of being a supervisor.
- Avoid discussing my personal life with the superior.
- Ask his or her views on the organization we work for.
- Share my future career plans with the superior.
- Ask for his or help, even when I really don't need it.

CONTRACTUAL FACTOR

Items included in the contractual factor describe the subordinate's conformity to formal role requirements, the superior's expectations, and general communication rules or conventions. Rule-following deference to the supervisor in respect to relational, organizational, and societal conventions are the central themes. The items included in this factor are:

- Be sure to follow the rules that have been established.
- Remain polite toward the superior.
- Respond with a positive attitude when a superior asks me to do something.
- Make sure I have a clear understanding of what my superior thinks my responsibilities are.
- Accept criticism from him or her openly.
- Keep his or her secrets confidential.
- Always stick by agreements we have made.
- Avoid the expression of extreme negative emotion toward him or her.
- Help my superior by influencing other employees in a positive way.

- Ask for his or her advice on work-related matters.
- Follow organizational rules as closely as possible to avoid problems with the superior.
- Be certain to follow his or her suggestions for doing the work.
- Avoid embarrassing the superior in any circumstances.
- Be honest in everything I say to him or her.
- Avoid conflicts with the superior.
- Schedule meetings with him or her to discuss work issues.
- Make sure I can be reached in person or by phone much of the time.
- Don't take the superior's criticism too seriously.
- Give my superior some of the credit when I do a good job.

While listed as two of the factors included above, avoiding the expression of extreme negative emotion toward the superior and avoiding contact with the superior did not show statistical significance, which could indicate that most people in the normative group did not see the avoidance of conflict as being necessarily a positive attribute.

REGULATIVE FACTOR

The regulative factor included tactics that appear to maintain the relationship by managing the contacts with the superior. Some of the items suggest a need to maintain the relationship by censoring or distorting messages and by carefully managing the impressions that one is making. There is also an overtone of strategic self-presentation and emotional control that characterized these items. The behaviors are avoidant and manipulative, both characteristic of strategic regulation of messages, impressions, emotions, and contacts with the superior. Regulative items include:

- Avoid delivering bad news to the superior.
- Sometimes stretch the truth to avoid problems with the superior.
- Make sure the superior is in a good mood before discussing important work-related matters.
- Avoid appearing too ambitious when we talk.
- Talk only superficially.

- Try to avoid asking for direction.
- Appear enthusiastic, even if I'm not.
- Avoid the expression of extreme positive emotions in his or her presence.
- Share my frustrations with co-workers rather than with the superior.
- Avoid direct criticism of the superior.
- Avoid surprising the superior.
- Provide evidence to him or her that I am a good employee.
- Overlook his or her comments that might change our relationship for the worse.
- Ignore his or her mood swings.

DIRECT FACTOR

The direct factor included items referring to the direct negotiation of the terms of the relationship and open discussion of perceived injustices deriving from the relationship. The items included in this category were:

- Speak up when I feel he or she has treated me unjustly.
- Explicitly tell the superior how I expect to be treated at work.
- Make it known when I am unhappy about something at work.
- Discuss openly any problems in my relationship with him or her.
- Frequently offer my opinions.
- Make sure he or she knows when I have been successful.
- Document discussions with him or her.

While all of these factors and the items associated with them need to be taken into account when developing a relationship with a superior within which the subordinate will exert influence, the research highlights the prominence of the personal factor. This suggests that although organizational roles and reporting relationships may be formally defined, the maintenance of these relationships may be partially achieved through frequent discussion of personal information outside of formal channels.

The contact with the superior through the informal network may prevent deterioration of formal relationships during periods of infrequent formal communication. A key issue, then, for anyone who would influence superiors, would be to encourage discussion of non-work issues. Through these discussions, the subordinate solidifies friendship ties while presumably adding stability and predictability to the formal authority relationship.

Over time, these contacts work to the advantage of the subordinate, because the more solid, informal relationship provides a springboard for taking more risk in the act of upward influence attempts and other potentially threatening communication. Even the regulative tactics appear to support the notion of approaching rather than avoiding the superior. Subordinates who gravitate in their behavior more toward the regulative factor may recognize that achievement of personal goals, including their ability to influence up, requires preservation of a functioning relationship. In order to achieve this relationship, they invest considerable effort to edit messages, avoid negative exchanges, and generally minimize problems in the relationship. It is clearly important to develop a relationship that places the subordinate in an "in-group" position. Because of limits of time and other resources, most executives do not have the time to distribute time, energy, and resources uniformly. For a variety of reasons based on both individual differences and interactive opportunities, superiors divide subordinates into two broad categories: in-group and out-group.

In-group subordinates are generally granted considerable latitude in negotiating their rules. They influence their employers more often without recourse to formal authority and provide opportunities for reciprocal influence. On the other hand, out-group members are subjected to behaviors specified in the organization's formal definition of authority relationships. Research also shows that in-group subordinates are apparently more likely to share their superior's determination of work priorities, are more satisfied with their jobs, are more loyal and less likely to leave the organization, and are judged to be better performers. Perhaps the most important issue, from the perspective of influence, is that in-group subordinates apparently have freedom to communicate with their supervisors outside of the formally prescribed channels about issues that are not directly related to work. In this way, the superior becomes part of the subordinate's informal network. Such informal communication results in a supervisor who is better informed about the subordinate, more knowledgeable about the circumstances influencing the subordinate's performance, and more inclined to develop friendship ties with the subordinate. All of these factors enhance the subordinate's ability to influence up.

INFLUENCING UP—GENDER DIFFERENCES

This brief discussion of the effect of gender on influencing superiors is included here because there appear to be some general assumptions about differences in approach to influence based on sex. In research we have conducted, this has not proven to be true.

One study conducted by Turner and Henzl concluded that psychological sex type was neither a precise predictor of tactic choice for influence, nor was it able to account for a meaningful amount of the variance of tactic choice. They further assert that employers and employees should not necessarily expect stereotypic behavior from women in the organization and conclude that, while it may be true that men and women do behave differently in the way they communicate, this difference in communicative behavior seems to be based on a complex set of variables that may include but not be wholly determined by biological sex.

One interesting finding in their study, however, is relevant to some aspects of our current discussion, and provides a tie-in with some previous observations. Women supervisors with male employees were found to use more assertive strategies than males supervising men, such as arguments, direct requests, or implied threats. They were also found to be less assertive with female employees than with males. Male employers with female employees use the tactic of exchange significantly less frequently. This may be a result of the growing sensitivity to sexual harassment issues. The notion of avoiding "exchange" behaviors seems to extend to the full range of compliance-gaining situations.

While it is probably not necessary to overemphasize a point, when a subordinate is attempting to establish a relationship that places the superior firmly in his or her informal network, sex differences may need to be taken into account. Because there are so many available stereotypes for male/female relationships within an organizational context, there is a danger that sex differences can be overemphasized to the detriment of the relationship. The best advice is probably this: while attempting to manage your superior, take the sex difference or similarity into account and then trust the stability of the influencing model. That is, regardless of sex, you are bound to have the greatest impact if you focus on the intrinsic, extrinsic, and strategic approaches to influencing up rather than attempting to trade on sexual differences or similarities based on stereotypes.[4]

INFLUENCING UP AND LOCUS OF CONTROL

An additional factor that seems to have some bearing on the various types of compliance-gaining activity that people employ when attempting to influence superiors is the concept of *locus of control*.[5] The theory of locus of control is a construct that distinguishes between people based on their orientation to the primary source determining the outcomes of their life. It divides people into two primary groups: internals and externals. The concept derives from the notion that individuals through a lifetime of social learning experience acquire a generalized anticipation about the source: a reinforcement for their actions.

People with an external orientation believe that rewards for their behaviors depend on luck, fate, and other factors over which they have relatively little control. Externals are more dependent on conventions and norms to order their uncertain world of chance and upon the authority behind these conventions, which is the arbiter of fate. In our style discussions, they fall more toward the control dimension and are most comfortable aligning themselves with a belief system.

On the other hand, internals tend to rely upon themselves and expect rewards as a consequence of their own actions. In our style discussions, internals would fall more toward the persuasion and vision categories. One researcher notes that people with high levels of internal locus of control are those who believe that they are responsible for affecting change in their environments, whereas their control counterparts feel that they are controlled by their environments.[6]

As with styles, the subordinate attempting compliance-gaining behavior with a superior is not the only person in the dynamic with a prevailing locus of control. From the perspective of the superior with an external locus of control, compliance-gaining behavior would be received more favorably when it is based on communication that fits with expectations, relates to consequences and the formal structure of organizational relationships, identification, and pre-acceptance of the point of view being presented. On the other hand, superiors with an internal locus of control would probably respond more favorably to appeals grounded in values on the intrinsic side and obligations on the extrinsic side, because internals tend to be less concerned with meeting other's demands, and more concerned with self-fulfilment. Some research suggests that internals in general are more resistant than externals to compliance-gaining attempts.[7] Individuals with an internal locus of control tend to be more successful than externals in influencing others.[8]

In general, people with external locus of control select strategies that are based on negative expectations and outcomes, while people with internal locus of control select strategies that are based on relationships, identification, values, and obligations.[9] While much of the research conducted in this area focuses on relatively specific responses under controlled conditions, what emerges is a pattern of behavior that suggests that an executive's ability to influence upward begins with a world view. This world view tends to place individuals with an internal focus in a better position than those with an external focus when it comes to influencing superiors. The world view of external locus of control places the subordinate at a disadvantage in the influencing situation because he or she carries negative expectations into the effort. At the very least, it is useful for anyone engaging in influence behavior—and in particular, influencing behavior aimed at a superior—to gain an understanding of their own tendencies with regard to locus of control.

Appendix C of this book includes a version of J. B. Rotter's *Locus of Control* scale. This scale consists of eleven paired statements, with one statement indicating external locus of control, the other indicating internal locus of control. A person scoring from zero to five on the scale would be demonstrating more internal locus behavior, while externals are defined by scores of six to eleven. The suggestion here is not that an individual scoring one way or another engage in efforts to alter their world view, but rather to carry an awareness of these tendencies into the influencing situation. Strategies are selected based on their context and effectiveness rather than predetermined expectations of outcomes.

There are other arguments in favor of accessing personal locus of control. Internals tend to report more job satisfaction than externals and seem to be significantly more satisfied with a participative supervisory style than externals. Externals tend to be more satisfied with direct supervision.[10]

MANAGING THE SUBORDINATE-SUPERIOR RELATIONSHIP—
WHOSE JOB IS IT?

In order to fit the challenge of influencing superiors in perspective, it is useful to look at what the broader patterns of influence are in an individual's network and how complex this pattern can become.

Figure 10.1 illustrates a hypothetical influencing pattern. The person at the center is ultimately responsible for exerting some degree of influence on all of the people in this hypothetical network. Solid and dotted

Figure 10.1
Patterns of Influence

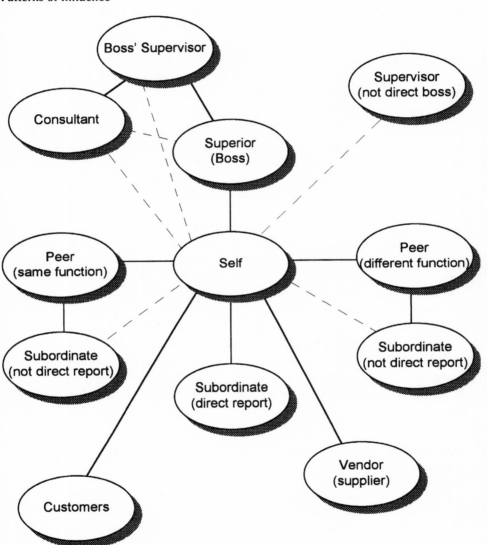

lines differentiate whether or not the relationship with the individual or group is direct or indirect. Dotted-line relationships do not suggest that the requirement for exerting influence or compliance-gaining behavior is any less. In fact, in some cases, it is more important for getting work done than the more direct relationships.

As John Gabarro and John Kotter pointed out in their classic article in the *Harvard Business Review*, "Managing Your Boss," managers and executives at any level need to recognize that a relationship with a superior involves mutual dependence, and if that relationship is not working effectively, they cannot be effective on their jobs. Most of us learn and solidify our approaches to dealing with superiors through our relationship with our parents. As a result, we develop one of two primary responses to being put in a subordinate position. We either tend to be acquiescent or tend to rebel. However, in the boss-subordinate relationship, because of the mutual dependency, the burden for managing that relationship falls more heavily on the subordinate than on the superior.[11]

The most effective managers in today's workforce are those who not only actively and effectively supervise subordinates' products, markets, and technologies, but also effectively manage the relationship with their superiors. One of the key factors in managing the relationship with the boss is to avoid the assumption that the superior will, somehow, know exactly what the subordinate needs at all times and have the ability to provide it. This notion is dangerously unrealistic.

Along with all the other aspects of a manager's career life, he or she must also make a point of seeking information and help from superiors as it is needed. This requires the application of influencing strategies. Effectively managing the relationship with a superior begins with an analysis of the compatibility and incompatibility between the subordinate and the superior. The subordinate needs to be honest about his or her preferences and priorities and ask the following questions.

- Are we similar in background, tastes, education, ways of facing life, and general values?
- Do I understand my superior's goals and objectives, both for the organization and on a personal level? If not, how can I find out?
- What obstacles and frustrations, both internal and external to the organization, are part of my superior's work-life?
- What is my superior's prevailing style and how does that style blend or conflict with my prevailing style?

- What are my superior's particular strengths and what opportunities can I present or develop in order for him or her to apply those strengths in my behalf?

- What are my superior's weaknesses and blind spots? How can I offset or mitigate the potential negative outcomes that may occur as a result of these shortcomings?

- What are my particular strengths and how can I present or develop opportunities to employ these strengths in my superior's behalf?

- Where are my areas of weakness and how can I effectively involve my superior in offsetting the potential negative effects of these weaknesses?

- Is my superior part of my informal network? If not, how can I go about developing our relationship along more informal lines?

Rosabeth Moss Kanter, talking about middle-managers as innovators, tells us that in order for managers to produce innovative achievements they must reach beyond the scope of their own particular job. Because they do not possess the power to carry out their own ideas, they must be able to acquire the cooperation of others when they need it. Therefore, creative managers are not empowered simply by their superior or their job; on their own they seek and find additional strength to carry out major new initiatives.[12]

By taking command of these initiatives, both personal and professional, managers in the middle can become corporate entrepreneurs, perhaps the most important players in today's business game. Part of this reaching out in the spirit of being an entrepreneur requires that they manage all of their relationships, including relationships with superiors.

NOTES

1. L. Schuster, "Walmart Chief's Enthusiastic Approach Infects Employees, Keeps Retailer Growing," *Wall Street Journal* (April 20, 1982): 21.

2. Vincent R. Waldron and K. J. Krone, "The Experience and Expression of Emotion in the Workplace: The Study of a Correction Organization," *Management Communication Quarterly* 4 (February 1987): 309.

3. Vincent R. Waldron, "Achieving Communication Goals in Superior-Subordinate Relationships: The Multi-Functionality of Upward Maintenance Tactics," *Communication Monographs* 58 (September 1991): 289–306.

4. Lynn H. Turner and Sally A. Henzl, "Influence Attempts and Organiza-

tional Conflict: The Effects of Biological Sex, Psychological Gender, and Power Position," *Management Communication Quarterly* 1, no. 1 (August 1987): 32–57.

5. A more comprehensive discussion of locus of control can be found in C. R. Berger, "Social Power and Interpersonal Communication," in *Handbook of Interpersonal Communication*, edited by M. L. Knapp and G. R. Miller (Newbury Park, CA: Sage, 1985), 439–499; M. J. Cody and M. L. McLaughlin, "The Situation as a Construct in Interpersonal Communication Research," in *Handbook of Interpersonal Communication*, 263–312; and L. R. Wheeless, R. Barraclough, and R. Stewart, "Compliance-Gaining and Power in Persuasion," *Communication Yearbook* 7 (1983).

6. Berger, "Social Power and Interpersonal Communication," 447.

7. P. E. Spector, "Behavior in Organization as a Function of Employee's Locus of Control," *Psychological Bulletin* 91 (1982): 482–497.

8. E. J. Phares, "Internal-External Locus of Control as a Determinant of Social Influence Exerted," *Journal of Personality and Social Psychology* 2 (1965): 642–647.

9. B. E. Goodstadt and L. A. Hjelle, "Power to the Powerless: Locus of Control and the Use of Power," *Journal of Personality and Social Psychology* 27 (1973): 190–196.

10. Bonnie E. Garson and Douglas J. Stanwyck, "Locus of Control and Incentive in Self-Managing Teams," *Human Resource Development Quarterly* 8, no. 3 (Fall 1997): 247–258.

11. John B. Gabarro and John P. Kotter, "Managing Your Boss," *Harvard Business Review* (January/February 1980): 92–100.

12. Rosabeth Moss Kanter, "The Middle Manager as Innovator," *Harvard Business Review* (July/August 1982): 95–105.

CHAPTER 11

The Influencing Group Process

It is logical that a chapter on facilitation follow chapters that concern themselves primarily with coaching subordinates and influencing supervisors. In the one case we are talking about helping the individual achieve goals and objectives as well as more productive and acceptable behaviors in the workplace. In the case of facilitation, we are also talking about helping others and in some cases this also pertains to their individual behavior patterns and performance ability. The major difference, of course, is that the focus of a facilitator is on group processes rather than on individual processes.

If you are the boss, it is easy enough to order your direct reports to move in a particular direction. In some cases, this may be exactly what is called for from you as a manager who needs to move quickly toward a decision or action that requires "all hands on deck" behavior from the people around you. However, as we have discussed elsewhere, in today's workplace, many of the groups that managers find themselves working with—and in fact leading—are not made up of direct reports; rather they are individuals in the organization who may be at the same or higher levels than the manager called upon to facilitate, and will not respond effectively to being ordered around.

The most effective facilitators are excellent influencers. They apply strategy, ingratiation, rational processes, and exchange of value as needed to help the group achieve an understanding by consensus and a commitment to action. A facilitator is not a presenter, does not dominate a group, does not actively block progress, or seek personal recognition. The role of facilitator calls for skill in a series of role behaviors such as:

- Initiator
- Information Seeker
- Clarifier
- Coordinator
- Energizer
- Procedure Developer

Being a good facilitator is different from being a good leader or a good manager. It requires a special set of skills and abilities. Think of trying to move a piece of string in a straight line—very difficult to push, but easy to pull.

Our focus here is on managing group process through the effective use of influencing behavior. One chapter cannot cover all of the various factors that go into successful facilitation. Indeed, that is the subject for another book.

Richard G. Weaver and John D. Farrell in their book *Managers as Facilitators* talk about one of the essential elements of facilitation being self-knowledge. They point out that good facilitators are aware of how they are perceived by the group, and how their presence exerts influence. Self-knowledge keeps the facilitator in touch with what his or her own preferences are for interacting with others. These preferences impact their general orientation, how they achieve results, and the actions they take to achieve those results. Personal preferences also can limit the type of information they need in order to make decisions. Keeping these personal preferences in focus enables good facilitators to guard against working through their own personal agendas, which may be contrary to what is best for the group.[1]

Few managers have the opportunity to act as pure facilitators. In the ideal, a facilitator is relatively unconcerned with content, that is, what the group needs to decide or act on. Professional facilitators are very often more effective at achieving results primarily because of their neutral status and the fact that they most probably won't be affected by the outcome, regardless of what the group decides or does. Managers, on the other hand, are not so fortunate as to be able to remove themselves entirely from the result of a group action. It often becomes necessary to step out of the facilitator role and enter into the process as a participant with a point of view as well as needs and concerns that need to be addressed. Short of actually entering into the foray, managers as facilitators also influence group outcomes strategically through the preparation and timing of agendas, by selection of group members when they have the option to do so, by presenting questions that focus the group's attention in a particular direction, and by rewarding or being unresponsive to certain suggestions and ideas that are not in line with the manager's preferred outcomes.

QUESTIONING TO STIMULATE AND CONTROL DISCUSSION

Whether the objective is a free and open exchange of ideas resulting in a decision that has a neutral effect for the manager-facilitator, or whether he or she needs to move a group in a direction that requires compliance to a set of predetermined objectives, the most important tools are the questions the facilitator asks. The best facilitators are those who ask questions rather than make presentations, those who listen more than they talk. Questioning is a powerful tool because it involves the group in the process of discovering their own needs and solutions. How one asks questions will guide that discovery. Questions are the facilitator's means of controlling the dynamics because questions have a very powerful influence on behavior and thought processes. Even when there is a clear agenda at the outset, questioning helps to involve the group in creating a solution, which in turn helps the facilitator gain commitment.

Research has demonstrated that the way a question is worded can significantly influence the response received, the completeness of the answer provided, and the impact the question has in terms of creating credibility and trust. Focusing on questions will help to

- gain important information
- control the interaction
- determine specific needs
- create a better understanding of the situation
- increase the perception of trust and credibility
- increase the probability of gaining a commitment
- explore all options

If one doesn't ask questions, one must make assumptions. Making assumptions is a dangerous strategy and often causes the facilitator to go off in directions inappropriate for the group, or creates additional obstacles to overcome.

Questions can be either open or closed. Open questions get the widest, richest range of responses. Closed questions require a "yes" or "no," up or down answer.

Open Questions

Open questions are questions that seek the group's opinions, feelings, plans, strategies, ideas, and the like on a variety of pertinent subjects. They uncover and help the group recognize and acknowledge needs, problems, and opportunities. Responding to open questions involves the group more directly in the process. Open questions encourage people to talk more freely about their needs and to provide important information about their motives and processes. This is particularly important in determining what influence strategy is going to be most effective with each of the members of the group in question. Also, it helps the facilitator identify potential allies.

Open questions always begin with expansive questioning words like "what," "why," and "how." They may also be constructed as statements, using phrases like "Tell me . . . ," "Let's talk about . . . ," or "Help me understand . . ." The difficulty most people have with open questions is not using enough of them. Insightful open questions can be great conversation starters, and the right open questions can do a great deal to improve the facilitator's credibility. Many managers, when placed in the facilitation role, have difficulty spontaneously framing open questions. They must make a conscious effort to frame questions in an open mode, particularly at the beginning of a questioning segment. In preparation for any meeting being facilitated by the manager, it is a good idea to write down several open questions, rather than depend on spontaneous generation of these questions when they are called for (see Table 11.1).

Open questioning does not come naturally to most people. When we learn language as children, rarely does anyone, particularly our parents, ask us open questions. Remember back to your childhood and see if you can come up with one instance where your mother turned to you and said, "Tell me how you feel about how dinner went this evening." Usually questions to children are phrased more like: "Are you hungry?"

Table 11.1
Open Questions

Open questions can be classified into three basic types:

Analytical questions	Questions that cause the group to look at issues critically and evaluate the various options available: *"Let's look at how these two approaches differ."*
Hypothetical questions	Questions that invite the group to better evaluate alternatives, various approaches, and risks as well as benefits: *"What if we closed the warehouse in Ohio and handled all Midwestern deliveries out of Indianapolis?"*
Reactive questions	Questions that solicit the group's opinions and feelings on events that have happened and subsequent results: *"How did you feel about combining both sales organizations immediately after the merger?"*

"Did you eat yet?" "Did you finish your mashed potatoes?" "Did you do your homework?" As a result, when called upon to ask questions, unless we think about it, most of us will automatically gravitate to a more closed mode of questioning.

Not all people are comfortable responding to open questions. If a group member has some conflict or emotional involvement with a particular subject area, or is suspicious of the facilitator or the purpose of a particular question, the response will not be extensive. One can determine immediately if the person is hostile or suspicious by the response. His or her response will usually take the form of a question that forces the facilitator to be more specific.

Here are some key things to remember about open questions:

- The relationship with the group can be enhanced if the right questions are asked by the facilitator.

- Open questions seek opinions, feelings, plans, strategies, and ideas on a variety of pertinent subjects.

- Open questions can serve as a very effective way of demonstrating and enhancing your credibility with your group and thereby increasing your influence.

- When asking open questions, a facilitator must take care not to respond before the questioning process is done. The most critical issues tend to surface at the end of the discussion.

Closed Questions

Closed questions can often be answered with a simple "yes" or "no," or with particular facts that are important to the situation. These are questions that direct the group to respond with a specific answer. A limited choice of alternatives can be provided from which the group can choose. Asking closed questions is generally thought of as more efficient at gaining specific information than is open questioning. By limiting the range of choices the facilitator can cover several fact-finding issues in a relatively short period of time.

Closed questions are very useful for verifying and confirming specific information obtained as a result of open questions. They can also be used to provide direction and set the stage for open questions to expand the value and the meaning of the facts uncovered. They may also be used to confirm agreement to proceed or acceptance of a suggestion that the facilitator may have made. Because of the narrow response range, there is a limited amount of information that can be obtained by using a closed question.

While closed questions are very important, many facilitators overuse them and find themselves interrogating the group rather than having a natural conversation. A short sequence of focused questions can orient the group to important things to think about. Closed questions are particularly useful to confirm agreement.

Specific advantages of closed questions:

- They are effective for getting specific factual information.
- The answers to closed questions are easy to systematize and analyze.
- As long as they relate to non-personal things, they are generally perceived as easy to answer.
- They are useful to clarify and confirm information derived from open questions.

Where self-disclosure is required, however, they can be perceived as more threatening than open questions.

Probing Questions

Probing questions help to clarify misunderstanding, uncover objections, and focus the group's interests and concerns. Probes are critical. Like archaeologists on a search for hidden treasure, probes remove layers of material in order to arrive at the information sought. Probes must fit the occasion.

There are two basic types: direct and neutral. Direct probes are simply questions that require a fuller response.

"What do you mean by . . . ?"

"Could you go into that more?"

"You must have a good reason for making . . ."

"Can you help me understand . . . ?"

"What happened then?"

"How did that happen?"

Neutral probes lead the group toward a fuller response. The facilitator is communicating an interest in additional information. Neutral probes such as "I see . . ." "Really?" "Uh-huh." "Hmm." "And?" can be an effective influencing strategy since they reinforce the facilitator's interest in a particular subject area that may be more in line with the direction that he or she wants to move the group.

One characteristic that distinguishes the skillful facilitator from the novice is the level of comfort with silence. Many people feel the need to fill every moment with noise, appropriate or otherwise. Silence is one of the best probing techniques. Use the universal need to fill silence with words to encourage group members to provide more information. Simply leave silent space that they may be compelled to fill with additional information. The use of silence is enhanced by appropriately applying a wide range of nonverbal behavior. A smile, a frown, a nod of the head, a raised eyebrow, and the like communicate an expectation for more information and will usually elicit a response from most groups.

Here are some things to remember about probing questions:

• They are used to dig deeper into a subject area rather than to open a new area.

- Too many direct probes in a sequence will appear threatening.
- The use of probes grows out of a felt need on your part for more information, or to indicate your support for a particular point of view.
- Use a variety of probes so that you don't sound repetitious or superficial.

Using Questions for Control

It takes a certain amount of discipline to frame what's on your mind in the form of a question rather than to make a simple statement of how you feel. However, there are several reasons not to make such a statement. First of all, if one is looking for support for a particular point of view, by stating the position openly and too early on in the process the facilitator runs the risk of arousing opposition and contentiousness among those who have alternate points of view, or are neutral but don't want to be pushed. Following are some questions that can be asked to move the group in particular directions without stating a particular point of view.

1. To call attention to a point that has not been considered: "Has anyone thought about the cost of adding personnel?"
2. To ask how strong an argument is: "How much are you willing to commit to the success of that plan?"
3. To get back on track: "I may be missing something, but how does this relate to the budget issue?"
4. To suggest compromise among members who disagree: "Let's take a fresh look at this. What merits do each of you see in the other's point of view?"
5. To suggest that it's time to move to another issue: "Would you all agree that we have covered the delivery issue?"
6. To call attention to potential problems: "What are we missing here?"
7. To register the amount of agreement: "Does anyone see a problem with this plan?"
8. To suggest that the group is not ready to take action: "Do we need to do some more work on this?"

9. To suggest that nothing will be gained by further delay: "What's stopping us from implementing this plan now?"

MANAGING GROUP PROCESS

Obviously the manager-facilitator can't go into a group center with blinders on. His or her ability to observe group behavior with some degree of accuracy and take actions to either enhance or mitigate a situation will determine how effective his or her influencing is. Among the factors that take place as part of group process, these six are perhaps the most important:

1. Group emotions
2. Personal agendas
3. Alternate influencers
4. Degree of cooperation
5. Trust
6. Sincerity

Each of these factors is discussed separately below with some observation points for you to look for.

Group Emotion

Ideas presented in any group setting have feelings attached to them. When a member of a group suggests something, there is always a degree of emotional investment in offering up that suggestion. Emotions are also generated by interactions among the members, due to agreement, disagreement, or general chemistry. Sometimes the topics themselves create a certain level of discomfort and produce a variety of individual emotional reactions.

People in group settings, unless they are therapy or support groups, rarely discuss emotions openly. Take the emotional temperature of your group by listening to the tone of voices, observing facial expressions, gestures, and other forms of nonverbal cues. Look for:

• anger, frustration, warmth, affection, excitement, boredom, defensiveness, or fear

- any attempts by group members to block the expression of feel-ings
- either blocked or expressed, emotions associated with specific members of the group or random and shared by all

Personal Agendas

Perhaps because of the business climate, the general ambiguity, and the exponential change we have discussed earlier, most people enter into a group situation cautiously. They are not always certain they want to be a part of a group, and they have a need to feel safe and secure. The facilitator may even find some initial resistance that is quite outspoken. Members of the groups a manager facilitates have either been assigned, or have made a decision on some level to become a member of the group. Once the decision is made, the person wants to be a full-fledged member. Membership inclusion for group members is the degree to which they are accepted by the group, and acceptance is a major concern for most people.

Individuals also have a need to feel effective and competent in a group. Insecurity about satisfying this need is at the root of many group power struggles. The manager can enhance his or her influence by publicly ingratiating him- or herself to the group members and acknowledging in advance what he or she perceives as their potential contribution.

Group members are also concerned about opening up and sharing personal values. Even when there is an understanding that developing closer relationships is necessary, each person has a need to maintain a comfortable distance. These needs form each participant's personal agenda. Belonging, competency, and closeness are the basic needs in a participant's personal agenda. Each of these personal agenda items must be met and kept in balance. When they are not being met, different pat-terns, comments, and issues will rise to the surface and prevent you from moving the action forward. Look for:

- people seeming to be outside the group.
- the forming of subgroups where two or three members may band together for a period of time during which they are consistently agreeing and supporting one another.
- comments such as "I don't want to be here" indicate inclusion concerns.

- comments such as "Let's discuss my agenda" indicate effectiveness concerns.

- overly polite comments indicate intimacy concerns.

- nonverbal behaviors are a good clue to personal discomfort or comfort about these three concerns. Frequently moving about, not making eye contact, pulling back physically, and folding arms often show noninvolvement.

Alternate Influencers

Sometimes a manager-facilitator will find him- or herself facilitating a group that contains members that have power—formally or informally—over other members of the group. These individuals should be considered as alternate influencers and every attempt should be made to develop them as allies. Powerful group members can move the group or hold it back. Sometimes alternate influencers are not even members of the group. They could be an absent member, a boss, or a competitor. Look for:

- which members appear to be high in influence. Who within the group do other members appear to listen carefully to? What are their positions in the organization?

- which members appear to be low in influence. Does the influence appear to shift at various times depending on the subject at hand?

- rivalry in the group. Does someone in the group covertly challenge your leadership, and if so, what affect is that having on other group members?

- what, if any, power or influence sources exist outside of the group that could affect the behavior of the individuals in the group.

Cooperation

It is basic to all group performance that a high level of cooperation has to exist in order for the group to be successful. Observation should center on how well the group seems to work together. Is the overall atmosphere of the group competitive, with a touch of hostility and defensiveness, or do people seem to cooperate and open up to other members, sharing ideas and appearing to value each other's contributions?

As a general rule, if you can create an atmosphere that is open and accepting, cooperation will more likely occur.

Cooperation also results when members of the group have defined their particular positions within the group. In a hostile atmosphere participants are not likely to take the risks needed to arrive at the best solutions. In order to create this atmosphere of cooperation, the facilitator needs to depend heavily on intrinsic influencing behaviors: model what he or she is looking for from the participants; take some risks about being open and self-disclosive; and demonstrate a willingness to take risk. Look for:

- the acceptance or rejection of ideas that are presented
- any members who tend to provoke or annoy others
- anyone expressing that they would rather do this on his or her own
- involvement and interest
- topics that are being avoided
- side-tracking or getting hung up on a topic that is not related to the specific task at hand
- signs of enjoyment or distaste with the process

Trust

In order for the group to function effectively and for the manager-facilitator to exert influence, there is a need for interpersonal trust and openness. Trust is required before people will cooperate. This is particularly true if the issues being discussed are values-based. A low trust-level group will avoid many topics and appear cautious and wary. An air of formality may pervade and occasionally humor in the form of negative wise-cracking may relieve the tension. Identify the level of trust in the group by observing the behavior of individuals. Look for:

- anyone who appears to be willing to take risks
- group members who are eager and assertive, or cautious, and unwilling to commit themselves
- people who appear to be relaxed without being lethargic

- the degree to which differences in opinion and feelings about issues are encouraged and tolerated

Sincerity

Often when people are placed into groups where they feel they either do not belong or it is a waste of time, they will go through the motions of participating without providing any substance. It is interesting how people can talk at each other without really communicating. The part of the communication that is usually missing in these cases is the listening. Even people who are highly conversant in a language are subject to "bypassing." Bypassing occurs when two or more people in a group ascribe different meanings to the same word. For the group to communicate successfully it is not important that everyone have the same definition for a word (although it is a help if they do), but that everyone knows what the others mean when they use a particular word.

Sincerity in group process derives from a willingness on the part of all of the participants to listen carefully to each other and to evaluate each others' ideas. Look for:

- frequent questions asked for clarification and confirmation
- group members who paraphrase their understanding of others' ideas
- whether there was a lot of nonverbal or head-nodding and other support behavior
- whether there were phrases like "What I hear you saying is . . .", "Could you run that by me again?" and "So if I understand correctly, this is where we are now on this."

CLOSING WITH A RISK ISSUE QUESTION

Every meeting should end with an understanding of what the group members should do to make their commitment level clear. Asking a risk issue question toward the end of the meeting is one good way of determining just what the current level of commitment is.

- "So I'm feeling good about this plan, but you are the ones who have to live with it. How are you feeling right now?"

- "Are you all comfortable that we have covered all the important issues?"

Having received confirmation that the group has accepted the facilitator's proposal or summary of what they developed as a group, it is time to ask for a commitment. To do this requires three steps:

1. Confirm the group's needs as you understand them.
2. Summarize the specific benefits that the group has accepted during the course of the meeting, and the ways in which those benefits satisfy the group's perceived needs.
3. Request the group's commitment to the plan.

Overall, how a manager conducts him- or herself as a facilitator will go a long way toward enhancing his or her intrinsic influencing behaviors. Group membership isn't always voluntary. But whenever people join groups, they do so because membership may help them achieve one or more goals. Sometimes there is a close relationship between the goals of the group as a whole and its individual members. However, individual members have other goals as well. There are basically two determinants of group success. The first is how the group analyzes problems and chooses and implements the best solutions. The second involves building and maintaining good relationships. The manager's role as a facilitator is central to accomplishing these determinants.

NOTE

1. Richard G. Weaver and John D. Farrell, *Managers as Facilitators: A Practical Guide to Getting Work Done in a Changing Workplace* (San Francisco: Berret-Koehler, 1997), 44.

Afterword

Since we began with a story, it seems that ending with a story is appropriate. So, here goes.

As it happened, the "Chicken Prince" who became king was an excellent ruler. Everything was going well in the kingdom. The crops were plentiful, the taxes were low and everyone lived in peace. However, there was little diversion or excitement to enrich the lives of the people. The King himself was bored. He asked his advisors for ideas, and one idea seemed like a great solution to the problem. He decided to have a festival with dancing, singing and an array of contests, culminating in an archery contest that would determine who was the best archer in the kingdom. For the next several months all of the hamlets in the kingdom had small contests to determine the best archer in their district who would be sent to the big event at court.

Finally, the festival began. For two weeks there was singing, dancing, wonderful food and drink, and the archers contested for the honor of being the finest archer in the kingdom. At the end one archer, Sir Henry Shaft, stood above the rest. He was given a medal, several horses and cows, and a sizeable piece of land, and was sent on a good will tour of the kingdom to demonstrate his prowess.

One day while Sir Henry was approaching a small village, he came upon a large barn. He was astounded to see that on the side of the barn there were a hundred small circles. In the exact center of each circle was an arrow! Sir Henry dismounted and studied the array. His heart was pounding. Whoever shot those arrows was truly the greatest archer in the kingdom; perhaps the greatest archer of all time!

As it happens in these stories, a peasant soon came wandering by on the road. Sir Henry accosted him, "Sirrah," he said, "Do you know the knight who shot those arrows? I must meet him and bow to his skill."

"Sir knight," said the peasant, "you don't understand, Igor shot those arrows, but . . ."

"I must meet this Sir Igor immediately to pay homage," said the knight.

"Most noble knight, Igor is a poor farmer."

"How does he come to have such skill?" Sir Henry cried.

The peasant rolled his hat in his hand and looked up at the knight and said, "You see, Sir . . . Igor shoots the arrows first and then draws the circles."

I hope our discussion about influence has stimulated your thinking about how to get things done in today's organizations. Unlike Igor, we need to draw our circles first, before shooting the arrows. In this sense, drawing circles means determining in advance:

- who our allies are or how to create allies when needed,
- the needs or wants of the targets of our influence,
- what we have to offer that meets these needs,
- how to select strategies that fit the individual and the situation,
- and, most of all, what we need to do to build or enhance the relationship with this person as another human being.

None of the techniques or strategies outlined in this book are magic arrows. They are designed to make your moment-to-moment judgments more effective—to help you become the influencing executive.

APPENDIX A

Networking Style Inventory

		Scoring					
	Yes	1	2	3	4	5	No
1. In order to be effective, staff managers need to remove themselves from the mainstream of the business.							
2. It is very important to anticipate the changing needs of staff.							
3. I prefer to do most of my planning in isolation.							
4. A good staff manager must have in-depth knowledge of the business.							
5. I see staff functions as non-aggressive aspects of the organization.							
6. I solicit input on issues affecting my department from staff at all levels.							
7. A staff manager responds primarily when a problem occurs.							
8. The successful project or program confirms the judgments of upper management.							
9. Too much input and participation from my staff can hinder my effectiveness.							
10. The best measure of any implementation is the extent to which it actually alters behavior.							
11. Opinion leaders from the line side tend to interfere with my function.							
12. For business success, I see training as the most important function after sales.							
13. A solution or product can be judged by its content and where it has been used before.							
14. I am concerned by the current emphasis on measurement and validation for all initiatives.							
15. I am very concerned about employee reactions to my ideas and programs.							

		Yes	Scoring					No
			1	2	3	4	5	
16.	An effective staff manager can shape the judgments of upper management.							
17.	Most follow-up programs are ineffective for the effort they require.							
18.	Any program must be supported by the participants' superiors in order to be successful.							
19.	I enjoy shopping for new approaches and offering them to my organization/clients.							
20.	A good manager reports on how problems were addressed.							

Scoring:

Total number of:

A. Odd-numbered questions (no □)   **B.** Even-numbered questions (see□)

1's	_____	x 1 =			1's	_____	x 1 =	
2's	_____	x 2 =			2's	_____	x 2 =	
3's	_____	x 3 =			3's	_____	x 3 =	
4's	_____	x 4 =			4's	_____	x 4 =	
5's	_____	x 5 =			5's	_____	x 5 =	

A Subtotal

Less B Subtotal

Total Score

B Subtotal

Networking Style Matrix

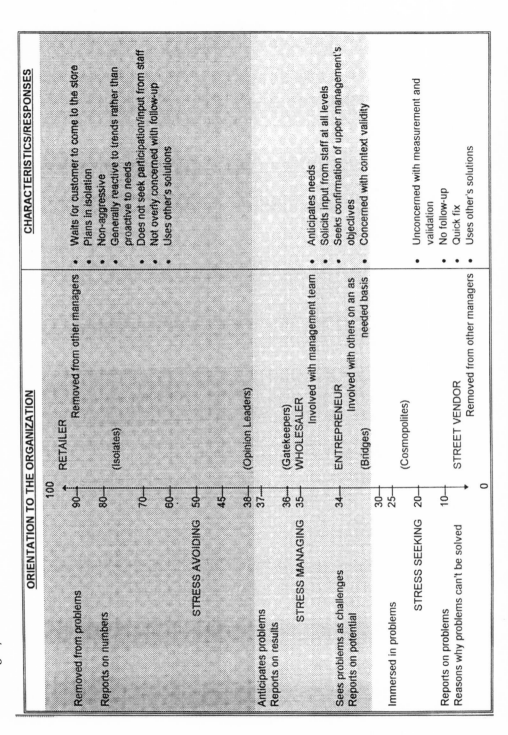

APPENDIX B

Building a Support Network

OVERVIEW

List your thoughts about the following questions.

1.   What kind of support would you most like to get from your co-workers?

- •   _____
- •   _____
- •   _____
- •   _____

2.   What kind of support would you most like to get from your superiors?

- •   _____
- •   _____
- •   _____
- •   _____

3.   The things I would like to change about my current support network are:

- •   _____
- •   _____
- •   _____
- •   _____

CURRENT NETWORK

For each category of network members listed below, provide the name of the person in your network who fits in that category and then make a judgment about your level of satisfaction.

Network Role	Person	Satisfaction			
		Unsatisfactory		Very Satisfactory	
		1	2	3	4
1. Business-related friends	_____ _____ _____ _____				
2. Professional advisors (consultants)	_____ _____ _____ _____				
3. Task helpers	_____ _____ _____ _____				

4. Professional groups and associations	_____ _____ _____ _____				
5. Challengers	_____ _____ _____ _____				
6. Supporters	_____ _____ _____ _____				
7. Access providers	_____ _____ _____ _____				
8. Mentors (models, teachers)	_____ _____ _____ _____				
	Total	__	__	__	__

SCORING:

Number of different
people listed   _____

Total of four columns   _____

Multiply the number of
people by the total for
columns   _____

384 and above	= very strong network
300 to 384	= good network
256 to 300	= room for improvement
200 to 256	= weak network
128 to 200	= rudimentary
128 and below	= no working network

IDENTIFY POTENTIAL NETWORK ALLIES

Function/Area/Department	Person(s)	Current Relationship
_____	_____	_____
	_____	_____
	_____	_____
		_____
		_____
_____	_____	_____
	_____	_____
	_____	_____
		_____
		_____
		_____
_____	_____	_____
	_____	_____
	_____	_____
		_____
		_____
_____	_____	_____
	_____	_____
	_____	_____
		_____
		_____
		_____
_____	_____	_____
	_____	_____
	_____	_____
		_____
		_____
		_____

ACTION PLAN

Person	*Action*

APPENDIX C

Locus of Control Questionnaire

The following pairs of statements describe some aspect of your job, yourself, and your experience at work. Read each pair of statements and place a mark in the space in front of the *one* that most accurately reflects your response to the statement. Do not omit any items and *never check both items*. (*indicates externality.)

1. _____   *Many of the misfortunes I encounter at work are mainly due to bad luck.

   _____   Most of the misfortunes I encounter at work result from mistakes I make.

2. _____   *Without the right breaks, one cannot be an effective leader.

   _____   Capable people who fail to become leaders have not taken advantage of their opportunities.

3. _____   Becoming a success is a matter of hard work, luck has little or nothing to do with it.

   _____   *Getting a good job depends mainly on being in the right place at the right time.

4. _____   When I make plans, I am almost certain that I can make them work.

   _____   *It is not always wise to plan too far ahead because many things turn out to be out of our control anyhow.

5. _____   *No matter how hard I try, sometimes my supervisor just doesn't appreciate me.

   _____   There is a direct connection between how hard I work and the evaluations I receive.

6. _____   In the long run, people in this company get the respect they deserve.

   _____   *Unfortunately, an individual's worth in this company often passes unrecognized no matter how hard he or she tries.

7. _____   In the case of the well-prepared employee there is rarely, if ever, such a thing as an unfair job assignment.

   _____   *Many times, job assignments tend to be so unrelated to training that preparation is really useless.

8. _____   Whether or not I get ahead at work depends mostly on my ability.

   _____   *Getting ahead at work often depends a great deal upon luck.

9. _____   *I have often found that what is going to happen, will.

   _____   Trusting to fate has never turned out as well for me as making a decision to take a definite course of action.

10. _____   *In the long run, the bad things that happen to individuals in this company are balanced by the good ones.

   _____   Most misfortunes individuals encounter in this company are the result of lack of ability, ignorance, or laziness.

11. _____   What happens to me at work is my own doing.

   _____   *Most of the time, I feel that I don't have enough control over the direction my career is going.

SCORING

Total score for * items: _____

0 - 5 = Internal locus of control.

5 - 11 = External locus of control.

Bibliography

BOOKS

Adler, Ronald B., and George Rodman. 1988. *Understanding Human Communication*. 3d ed. New York: Holt, Rinehart and Winston.

American Management Association. 1997. *Corporate Job Creation, Job Elimination, and Downsizing: Summary of Key Findings*. 1997 AMA Survey. New York: AMA.

Barnard, Chester. 1938. *The Functions of the Executive*. Cambridge, MA: Harvard University Press.

Bartlett, Christopher A., and Sumantra Ghoshal. 1989. *Managing Across Borders: The Transnational Solution*. Boston: Harvard Business School Press.

Benjamin, Alfred. 1969. *The Helping Interview*. Boston: Houghton Mifflin.

Berger, C. R. 1985. "Social Power and Interpersonal Communication." In *Handbook of Interpersonal Communication*, edited by M. L. Knapp and G. R. Miller. Newbury Park, CA: Sage: 439–499.

Cialdini, Robert B. 1993. *Influence: The Psychology of Persuasion*. Rev. ed. New York: Quill, William Morrow.

Cody, M. J., and M. L. McLaughlin. 1985. "The Situation as a Construct in Interpersonal Communication Research." In *Handbook of Interpersonal Communicaton*, edited by M. L. Knapp and G. R. Miller. Newbury Park, CA: Sage: 263–312.

Cohen, Allan R., and David L. Bradford. 1990. *Influence without Authority*. New York: Wiley.

Conrad, Charles. 1994. *Strategic Organizational Communication: Toward the Twenty-First Century*. 3d ed. Fort Worth: Harcourt Brace College Publishers.

Cummings, H. Wayland, Larry W. Long, and Michael L. Lewis. 1987. *Managing*

Communication in Organizations: An Introduction. 2d ed. Scottsdale, AZ: Gorsuch Scarisbrick.

Davis, Brian L., Carol J. Skube, Lowell W. Hellervik, Susan H. Gebelein, and James L. Sheard. 1992. *Successful Manager's Handbook: Development Suggestions for Today's Managers.* Minneapolis: Personnel Decisions, Inc.

Davis, Stanley M., and Paul R. Lawrence. 1977. *Matrix.* Reading, MA: Addison-Wesley.

Eccles, Robert G., and Nitin Nohria. 1992. *Beyond the Hype: Rediscovering the Essence of Management.* Boston: Harvard Business School Press.

Fairhurst, Gail, L. Edna, and Robert Sarr. 1987. *Manager-Subordinate Control Patterns and Judgments about the Relationship.* Communication Yearbook 10, edited by Margaret McLaughlin. Beverly Hills, CA: Sage.

Frank, Jerome D. 1961. *Persuasion and Healing: A Comparative Study of Psychotherapy.* New York: Schocken Books.

French, John R., and Bertram Raven. 1959. "The Bases of Social Power." In *Studies in Social Power,* edited by D. Kartwright. Ann Arbor: University of Michigan Press.

Gottlieb, Marvin. 1986. *Interview.* New York: Longman.

Gottlieb, Marvin R., and Lori Conkling. 1995. *Managing the Workplace Survivors: Organizational Downsizing and the Commitment Gap.* Westport, CT: Quorum Books.

Gottlieb, Marvin, and William J. Healy. 1990. *Making Deals: The Business of Negotiating.* New York: New York Insitute of Finance.

Kreps, Gary L. 1986. *Organizational Communication: Theory and Practice.* New York: Longman.

Madison, D. L., Robert Allen, Lyman Porter, Patricia Renwick, and Bronston Mayes. 1983. "Organizational Politics: An Exploration of Managers' Perceptions." In *Organizational Influence Processes,* edited by R. W. Allen and L. W. Porter. Glenview, IL: Scott, Foresman: 455–474.

March, James. 1970. "The Technology of Foolishness." In *Ambiguity and Choice in Organizations,* edited by James March and Johann Olson. Bergen: Universitetsforlaget.

Maslow, Abraham H. 1954. *Motivation and Personality.* New York: Harper & Row.

McCall, Morgan W., Jr. 1978. *Power, Influence, and Authority: The Hazards of Carrying a Sword.* Technical Report 10. Greensboro, NC: Center for Creative Leadership.

Minnick, Wayne C. 1957. *The Art of Persuasion.* Boston: Houghton Mifflin.

Monroe, Allan H., and Douglas Ehninger. 1967. *Principles and Types of Speech.* Glenview, IL: Scott, Foresman.

Murray, H. A. 1938. *Explorations in Personality.* New York: Oxford University Press.

Porter, Lyman W., Robert W. Allen, and Harold L. Angle. 1983. "The Politics of Upward Influence in Organizations." In *Organizational Influence Processes,* edited by R. W. Allen and L. W. Porter. Glenview, IL: Scott, Foresman: 408–422.

Raven, B. H. 1974. "The Comparative Analysis of Power and Influence." In *Perspective on Social Power,* edited by J. T. Tedeschi. Chicago: Aldine.

Rogers, Everett, and Rekha Argawala-Rogers. 1976. *Organizational Communication.* New York: Free Press.

Thompson, Victor. 1967. *Modern Organizations.* New York: Knopf.

Tiger, Lionel, and Robin Fox. 1971. *The Imperial Animal.* New York: Holt, Rinehart and Winston.

Tushman, M. L. 1983. "A Political Approach to Organization: A Review and Rationale." In *Organizational Influence Processes*, edited by R. W. Allen and L. W. Porter. Glenview, IL: Scott, Foresman: 393–407.

Weaver, Richard G., and John D. Farrell. 1997. *Managers as Facilitators: A Practical Guide to Getting Work Done in a Changing Workplace.* San Francisco: Berrett-Koehler.

Wilmot, W. W. 1980. *Dyadic Communication.* 2d ed. Reading, MA: Addison-Wesley.

ARTICLES

Cohen, Michael, James March, and Johann Olson. 1972. A Garbage-Can Model of Organizational Choice. *Administrative Science Quarterly* 17: 2–32.

Dansereau, F., G. Graen, and W. J. Haga. 1975. A Vertical Dyad Linkage Approach to Leadership within Formal Organizations: A Longitudinal Investigation of the Role-Making Process. *Organizational Behavior and Human Performance* 13: 46–78.

Davis, W., and J. R. O'Connor. 1977. Serial Transmission of Information: A Study of the Grapevine. *Journal of Applied Communication Research* 5: 61–72.

Falbe, Cecilia, and Gary Yukl. 1992. Consequences of Managers Using Single Influence Tactics and Combinations of Tactics. *Academy of Management Journal* 32: 638–652.

Gabarro, John B., and John P. Kotter. 1980. Managing Your Boss. *Harvard Business Review* (January/February): 92–100.

Garko, Michael. 1992. Persuading Subordinates Who Communicate in Attractive and Unattractive Styles. *Management Communication Quarterly* 5: 289–315.

Garson, Bonnie E., and Douglas J. Stanwyck. 1997. Locus of Control and Incentive in Self-Managing Teams. *Human Resource Development Quarterly* 8, no. 3 (Fall): 247–258.

Goodstadt, B. E., and L. A. Hjelle. 1973. Power to the Powerless: Locus of Control and the Use of Power. *Journal of Personality and Social Psychology* 27: 190–196.

Imperato, Gina. 1997. Harley Shifts Gears. *Fast Company* (June–July): 105.

Kanter, Rosabeth Moss. 1982. The Middle Manager as Innovator. *Harvard Business Review* (July/August): 95–105.

Kim, Young, and Katherine Miller. 1990. The Effects of Attributions and Feedback on the Generation of Supervisor Feedback Message Strategies. *Management Communication Quarterly* 4: 6–29.

Kipnis, David, Stuart M. Schmidt, and Ian Wilkinson. 1980. Intraorganizational Influence Tactics: Explorations in Getting One's Way. *Journal of Applied Psychology* 65, no. 4: 440–452.

Lee, M. B., and W. L. Zwerman. 1975. Developing a Facilitation System for Horizontal and Diagonal Communication in Organizations. *Personnel Journal* 54: 400–407.

Liu, W., and R. Duff. 1972. The Strength of Weak Ties. *Public Opinion Quarterly* 36: 361–366.

Madison, Dan, Robert Allen, Lyman Porter, Patricia Renwick, and Bronston Mayes. 1980. Organizational Politics. *Human Relations* 33: 79–100.

Maslow, Abraham H. 1943. A Theory of Human Motivation. *Psychological Review* 50: 370–396.

———. 1948. Some Thoeretical Consequences of Basic Need Gratifications. *Journal of Personality* 16: 402–416.

Phares, E. J. 1965. Internal-External Locus of Control as a Determinant of Social Influence Exerted. *Journal of Personality and Social Psychology* 2: 642–647.

Regan, Dennis T. 1971. Effects of a Favor and Liking on Compliance. *Journal of Experimental Social Psychology* 7: 627–639.

Schenck-Hamlin, William, Richard L. Wiseman, and G. N. Georgacarakos. 1980. A Model of Properties of Compliance-Gaining Strategies. *International Communication Association Convention*. Acapulco, Mexico, May 1980.

Schuster, L. Walmart Chief's Enthusiastic Approach Infects Employees, Keeps Retailer Growing. *Wall Street Journal* (April 20, 1982): 21.

Spector, P. E. 1982. Behavior in Organization as a Function of Employee's Locus of Control. *Psychological Bulletin* 91: 482–497.

Tolman, E. D. 1938. The Determiners of Behavior at a Choice Point. *Psychological Review* 45: 1–41.

Turner, Lynn H., and Sally A. Henzl. 1987. Influence Attempts and Organizational Conflict: The Effects of Biological Sex, Psychological Gender, and Power Position. *Management Communication Quarterly* 1, no. 1 (August): 32–57

Victor, Bart, and Richard Blackburn. 1987. Determinants and Consequences of Task Uncertainty. *Journal of Management Studies* 18: 108–132.

Waldron, Vincent R. 1991. Achieving Communication Goals in Superior-Subordinate Relationships: The Multi-Functionality of Upward Maintenance Tactics. *Communication Monographs* 58 (September): 289–306.

Waldron, Vincent R., and K. J. Krone. 1987. The Experience and Expression of Emotion in the Workplace: The Study of a Correction Organization. *Management Communication Quarterly* 4 (February): 287–309.

Wheeless, L. R., R. Barraclough, and R. Stewart. 1983. Compliance-Gaining and Power in Pursuasion. *Communication Yearbook* 7.

Wiseman, Richard L., and William Schenck-Hamlin. 1981. A Multidimensional Scaling Validation of an Inductively-Derived Set of Compliance-Gaining Strategies. *Communication Monographs* 48 (December): 251–270.

Index

About the Author

MARVIN R. GOTTLIEB is President of The Communication Project, Inc., a consulting firm based in Greenwich, CT. For more than twenty years as a management development specialist and trainer for consulting, manufacturing, travel, and financial services companies worldwide, Dr. Gottlieb has been at the forefront of computer-based distance learning instructional design. He has also completed a thirty-year career as Associate Professor of Communication at Lehman College–CUNY. Among his recent books is *Managing the Workplace Survivors* (Quorum, 1995, with Lori Conkling).